Hyster

Alex. Hami.

Hasterics, yi talk naboot? Ah see na coupla casiz whinAh wiz daein ma squerrbash noan Natiunil Service. Thir wiz wan guy – a wee Scouse, e wiz – thit wiz fuckn terrafy da baynits. N chrise, dae Ah mean terrafied. E seemed tae could dae enihi nelse thit wiz require dae im withoot bat na neyelid: fuckn tigir e wizinunarmed combat, ur hingnan swingn lik a narangatang oan thi parillel baur zur thi jungl net san that.

Bit eniwey. Wan day – e wiza cocky wee bastirt inaw, know whitAh mean? Fulla fuck noozn fuckn pride izif e'd drang kup thi piss oota that fuckn Mersey, jiss so ze could spew itaw upn wallow init whin e goat hamesick in thi barrack san that.

Wan day – in thi coursa palite, genaril convirsatiun – e tells me n Big Tam Ruthirfurd thit Glasgow za fuckn slag heap, na course, we jiss comes back aboot Livirpool be na nIrish middin – ur sumhn lik that. Jiss yir normil kinna bantir, thit go zoan tae pass thi time whin yir peeln spud zur dubbinin boot surenihn mineliss. Bit see sumae yir Inglish, but? Jeeziz! They jiss doant know whin a jokesajo kinit's time tae cry halt, kiz yir get norr thi line fae thi broad skirmish tae thi persanil battil, wi a ninsult thit jabs too deep.

So. This cunt cum zaway wi sumhn likif Livirpool za goo dIrish stronghole, dit's kizaw thi Oringe bastirts thit rule thi North – n that includes thi City a Glasgow, by thi way – iv been drow voota his toon kiz thiraw too lazy tae dae a day's wurk. Ur sum crap lik this.

Course, me n Tam says sumhn tae thi affect thitit soanlie papish rats thit could poassibli go oan liv nina tosspot lik Livirpool. No thit eni a thi baithae us izivir be nin thi fuckn place – bit that's baeside the point, izyi know, ineni gemm wherr yir scoren point san that. Nif wi couldiv lef titit that – nice n broad wi nuthn persanil ur that thit yi could adentafy wi – it wida been jiss tanuthir fitbaw match fur recriatiun, wi back tae wurk n normaliti eftir thi whissil hid went fur full time. Bit izAh say, this wee Inglish cunt? Know whit e says? Chrise, yiz couldnae guess fAh gie dyiza hunnir year, neethir yiz could. Wee papish bastirt, thit e wiz! E cum zaway wi:

Glasgow? e goes. *Glasgow? Ah'd drapa fuckn bomb oanit, so Ah wid – n nivir mine thi poor cathlics thit's therr. Aw thitid happin tae theym is, thid get thir riwar din hun a few year earliurn thir gonnae getit eniwey. Aye, n thir pleasure'd be fuckn dubbil tit be nup therr oan thi right hauna thi lor dan watchn thir proddy neighbours bein cass doonintae thi consumn fire za hell: awina fuckn wannir! A whole fuckn city a fuckn protistints. Five hunnir fuckn thoosn da thi bluenose bastirt – sur whitivir thi parfuckncentidge is – aw getn simulfuckntaneously kindem tae ivirfucknlastn perditiun, ina singil fell swoopa davine fuckn justice! Sweet jeeziz: **Ah'd** press that buttin*

2

then jum pintae thixplosiun, so Ah wid – it'd be fuckn hiv nitsel, jisstae see you zOringe cunts fryn furivir!

Well. Chrise, see vindictive? N see that Inglish fuckn whine ae a fuck naccent? Ah jiss couldnae help masel.

Scuse me a minnit, wull yiz? Ah goes tae Tam n this wee cunt, nAh get supn walk sorr tae wherr ma gear's parkt baeside ma bed. Ah kin hear thi Scouse stull rabbit noanin thi backgrunn, n stull in that nasal fuckn nambyfucknpambyfuckn *miaooow* – nifAh'd thoat Ah wiz mibbe gonnae think twicet, him gaunoananoananfucknoan jiss fuckn done fur us. Ah pick sup ma rifil, unclasps thi baynit fae wherr Ah'd lef tit oan thi barril, n tiptoe zup baehin thi Scouse's heid n nod zacroass tae Big Tam.

Aye, goes Tam, getn ma drif tan keep nim gaun, *funny thing is, but, wir no aw protistint sin Glasgow, cunty – me, frinstince!*

N quickizanarchbiship stick nit upa passn choirboay, e thro zoot baith fist san coups thi wee bastirt owir thi fit Ah've goat stretch toot baehine dim.

Crash! e goes.

Backwurds, right flat ootoan thi flerr – nafore e zevin realised wherr e izur how e's goat therr – Tam's goatiz feet, Ah'm sit noaniz erims croass towir iz chiss, tanAh'm force niz chin back wi ma lef haunin … stroke niz throat wi thi baynit in ma right.

Well. Wi didnae know whit e wiz gonnae dae, didnae know jiss how e wiz gonnae riac, bitAh sippose … Ah sippose sumhn lik – him thresh naboot, scream nobscenatiz, shoutn fur mercy nshite niz pants, hid went through ma mine. Ah mean, aw wi hid intendit wiz giein thi cunt a real good bouta thi skittirz, thit wid mibbe may kim watchiz fuckn moo thin future.

Well, it certinli hid thi dasire daffec tawright – bitit gie duz a helluva fuckn fright inaw, so it did.

See that? E goes lik that fuck nerima mines, thi wey Ah'm haudnit wi ma haun clenched. Rigid. Fuckn motiunliss. Away ina wee, smilin dwam n sterr nit sweet fuckaw.

That'll soart yi oot, ya wee Livirpool bastirt, yi! Tam's shoutn, twistn thi poor swine's fit izif e's tryn tae screw it right aff. *Caw yirsel a cathlic, ya cunt? Yir no eve na fuckn Christiun!*

Naw, Ah goes, *hingoana minnit, Tam.*

Kiz sitnupit thi ta pen, dAh could see thi buggir's face fae wherr Tam couldnae – nAh wiz merrn jiss ta wee bit sirprise dit thi lacka risponse wi wir getn tae aw wir kine dattentiuns.

Stoapa minnitn cumup here. Sumhn zrang. Thir sumhn no right. Ah think thi bastirt's went intae a fit.

Well, jeeziz wir we worried? Thir wiz nuthn wi could dae thit wid way kimup. Wi shoo kim; wi talk titim; wi blew oaniz face; wi pullt im tae iz feet – bit e couldnae staun. Jiss fell owir n killaps tintae wir erim zizwi stood therr haudnimup. *Jeeziz*, Ah wiz sayn tae masel iz wi lay dim doonoaniz bed, *wirinfurit noo, awright – though chrise knows whit thi charge'll be. Fuckn brainslaughtirur sumhn.*

Wir jiss staunin therr, orr thi tapae im n lookn doon, scratchn wir heid zan shiten fuckn bricks, when suddinli Tam freezes then reachizowirn grab za haudae ma shoodir.

Lissn, Wullie, e goes, *whit's that? Sum cunt's fuckn march inup thi fuckn path!*

Wi lookit each uthir, bowilz gaunizif wid jiss tetta packit a All Bran droont in Mulka Magnesia n prune juice, n thigithir wi belt orr tae thi windae n cray noot. It's thi fuckn sergeant! Aniz goosestepnit straight furoor billit, izif thi cunt's smell na six month sentince cookinup baehine wir door.

Jeeziz chrise! Ah goes, jiss loassn thi ragawthifuckngithirit thi thoatae it. *Get up, ya Inglish, fuckn slag, yi!*

Ah run zowir n ben zorr thi tapae im, get sa haudae iz lapel zan gie zimiz hefti a fuckn shake iz that Laziris mussta goat tae bringim back fae thi landa thi deid.

Way kinup, wull yi, ur yill hivuzn fuckn dock, ya cathlic bastirt, yi!

N bae this time, Ah'm stoat niz heidupndoonaffa thi pilla in time tae they bastardn boots, n me n Tam's jile sentince getn nearirn fuckn nearir wi ivri fuckn step!

Chrise!

Tam's stullit thi windae, davide nizattentiun baetween swivlln roon tae watch how Ah'm get noan wi thi Scouse, n guagen how long wiv goat afore Threestripe sit thi fuckn doorhaunil.

E zoan thi step, Wullie, e zoan thi step – gie thi bastirt a belt in the fuckn chops!

Aw, fuck me! Ah go, zin sheer fuckn sweatn desparatiun. *In fura fuckn penny…!*

NAh opins ma haun, aim zitup n take sa right good fuckn swipe itim – **slap!** oan thi cheek.

N jeeziz – didit no wurk!

Ah mean, when yi thing kabootit in thi clear lighta day, thi shockae it couldiv knoackt thi bastirt right intae kingdumfuckncum nuz intae clink for life. Bit whit wi dunin thi spurra thi momint turn doot tae be thi salutiun yir fuckn heidshrinkirs wida cherged yi haufa year's wages fur.

Thi Inglish cunt opin zizeyes, see zizsel lie noan thi bed wi me peern doonitimn sweatn bloodn kay sAh've killt im – n e pull zizsel backup thi metil heidboard n spits:

Whit's gaunoan here, ya big Scotch poof, yi!

Chrise.

Ah wiz that rilieve, dAh fell'doonoan thi tapae thi nix bedn, whin Tam shout sacroass baetween gasp sa breath n fuckn laughtir thit thi sergeant's walk toan tae thi nix hut – that poor fucknInglindir musstiv thoat e wizina fuckn loony bin!

See hasterics? Doan't talk tae me aboot hasterics.

If me n Big Tam didnae hiv hasterics that eftirnin – Ah widnae like tae see enicunt thit did.

Alex. Hamilton

Maureen Sangster

First Visit to Dunfermline

snow
barely noticeable
lands on the neck of a gargoyle
whose home is the Town House wall

even on the cold grey stone
of the gargoyle's thick extended neck
the first few snowflakes melt

it's the same for these snowflakes
landing on the Abbey wall
they melt too, they have possessed
a shorter life than the dead buried here

but the wind, for once, dies down
the Bridges in the distance stand
strangely-shaped skeletons

they wait for flesh to clothe them
it is snow that falls

snow flooring doorways
snow turning hilly streets into ski-slopes
snow creating a pointy hat on top
of the gargoyle's glowering head

snow settling in necklaces
down the green coppery spire in the distance

snow making sure the Park shrubs
are wrapped up well in white –
their new school uniform

snow zinging in snowballs in playgrounds
snow getting free rides
on the top of the red-and-cream Fife buses

snow, no longer dreaming of a landing,
worrying about a welcome, but
snow
covering all there is to know and see in Dunfermline.

The Moon's Leopard

the moon's leopard prowls tonight
feet through vapoury gleaming light
the moon's leopard looks for clues
for where Tom has gone to
Tom   Tom

as though hanging memories on the line
it seems we mourners are coping fine
really we look for God or Death
when there's only the moon's leopard's breath
Tom   Tom

in the forest of the leopard's mind
by the glaciers he left behind
in the fiery clearings made
everywhere – Tom's body was laid
Tom   Tom

the moon's leopard finds glass
in a round white ball on the fabulous grass
the leopard's tongue licks the cool
surface the glass ball becomes a pool
Tom   Tom

here Tom lies here Tom swims
first he's one, then there's many hims
sad delight but magnificent sight
the moon's leopard brings us Tom tonight
Tom   Tom

Fiona Girvan

Awful Kirkcaldy Baby

Awful Kirkcaldy baby
I pity you
with your square doughy face
and the life you lead
submerged in pram or push-chair beneath
the very frilled weight of
                 excessive coverings

Euch! your regal outings
cut no iced cake with me
You are an anachronism in 1992
boy in blue
girl in pink

& then a little older
you trot overdressed
with granny to the shops
a little girl gazing into
her gleaming black patent shoes
having to guard against dirt
on her white socks
the collar is round your neck
lacy enough

There is marriage ahead of you
swaddling of your own infants
& many washes on the whites cycle
of your automatic
Babies bundles of pride
while your life drips
like the tap you leave
for your husband to fix

that boy in blue
that boy in grubby blue
brought on to do
what men should do

Maureen Sangster

Else

Maggi Higgins

Else arrived fifteen minutes late for her Mum, and sent Les in to draw for a while in the front room.

"It's still going on, Mum."

"What was it this time?" Her Mum lit a cigarette.

"I don't know, a bit like… you know those ladders they use to clean upstairs windows? It was like them being set against the wall, and someone was stampin' up them! I checked everywhere again, but there was no one around and the kids slept through it again. Them downstairs hear nothin', but they sleep at the back."

Her Mum addressed her father.

"What do you think, Phil?" There was an awkward pause as he examined his fingers closely, but said nothing. His wife became more insistent.

"I mean it's no right Elsa being by herself with this. I don't like it, maybe she should come here?"

This was more ominous than coping with the poltergeist, or whatever it was. Else felt that the Beastie would probably be warmer-natured, and certainly less threatening, than her Mum.

"No, don't be silly. God, after five years bein' thrown out of houses, I'm sure as hell fightin' for this one! Anyway I'm off to do my picture."

Her Dad at last found voice. "Have you heard from Housing Benefit?"

"Phil! For God's sake, you asked her that yesterday!"

"It's okay Mum. Look I'm sorry, I'll phone later, you know what they're like." She owed her Dad three months' rent, and it wasn't fair! I mean he had to retire because of his nerves and now he was worryin' about money because of her. It was fuckin' demeanin' … she was 29 years old for Chrissake. She'd better go, although she knew her Mum would give him a hard time when she left … the poltergeist became the lesser of the two evils.

Once back in the house her energy wavered. God she felt down, an' there didn't really seem much point in tidyin' up … apart from the weans, no one would see it. Well, she had to finish the picture. It was comin' on, but she couldn't see the eyes… it was a problem.

She tried the phone. It rang…

"Hello, I wonder if you could help me. I'm a student and I applied for Housing Benefit three months ago… sorry?… Elsa Leadbetter, 51 Keir Crescent… yes I'm on Income Support… but they told me to phone you in a couple of days… somebody from your office. I don't… Look they're on strike! Why can't you… Thanks very much for the help!" Elsa slammed the phone down and tried to stop crying. Some days there was just no point. She heard the post and ran down, but it was just a letter from the Electricity. She carefully filed it away. How could she work? She'd thought that it might have been from one of the publishers. Maybe she should go out, sit in the sun, but she knew she wouldn't.

The picture waited, with eyes that couldn't see. It would make a beautiful sculpture… but that would cost too much, besides she'd never done it before. But the eyes wouldn't matter then. She was tired, there was no point and she lay on the bed and closed her eyes.

The passages narrowed in front of her, one tiny chamber leading to another, and finally into a low-ceilinged room. All round the room were dusty old lamps which she knew instinctively wouldn't work. Where was the phone? The only light was from a low window which backed onto another tenement wall. Else wanted out. She wanted to go back, but as she approached the door a man appeared at the doorway. She struggled. For a moment she seemed to gain consciousness, and willed her arm to move, her body to sit up. She felt drugged, quite ill in fact, and started to slide back into the darkness…

He was very dark, malign if there was such a thing, and the only way out was by him. As she came closer he grew huge. The door widened with him. Softly she began, "Our Father, who art in heaven…"

He laughed. "It only works if you believe, and you don't believe, Else!"

The fright made him stir again, and semi-conscious she prayed for God's help. She could see the time, the bedside lamp, the familiar picture that had no eyes. She commanded her body to rise, but her limbs seemed caught.

The prayers seemed to be helping. He had shrunk and was almost normal size now.

"I know that you're a dream, that you can't harm me!"

He moved, as if on wheels, backwards into the passage. Else forged on although she was scared, not daring to give him a fighting chance. As each chamber was passing he grew smaller, fainter. She grew in assurance.

She woke again, as frightened of the paralysing fear that stopped her from breaking out of the nightmare as she was of the Thing itself. This time was for real though, and she got up.

Sittin' on the edge of the bed she tried to think what to do. This was about the fourth time this had happened. Normally Else couldn't sleep at night, never mind during the day, but now she felt drugged all the time. Maybe she was losing the place! She was scared to go back to the Doctor. That last time he'd just said that everyone gets one chance, one cry for help. And to be fair, over the years, with the beatings an' all that, she'd used her's up.

Maybe she could tell him there was a difference between attacks from others, and the ones from inside your head. Maybe she could say that one caused the other. It was no use, she couldn't go down to the surgery with this one. They'd lock her up. Besides, what if they took the children away …you read these things. For Christ's sake, now she really was losin' her marbles! She needed a break. Not a rest 'cause she couldn't do that, but a break would be good. How the hell could she get a break when she couldn't live? She looked at the paintings all around her. She'd been offered enough for them, and she'd never been anywhere. Just to see Paris, or maybe Rome. But she was building a portfolio for an exhibition. That's what she told everyone. Really she was scared to sell them. They were all she had, she was scared she could never work again. Och, her head was a mess! The tears started to roll again, but she knew that it wouldn't last, it would stop soon.

Back down the road for Les, and Greg would be back as well. Her Mum was worried when she saw her, asked her to stay for tea, but she no longer allowed herself that kind of escape, and went back straight away. Funny, she could never really think what home would be like. She had never stayed long enough anywhere.

The kids asked about the picture. They were both good at art. She hoped they wouldn't do it when they grew up though. She wouldn't stop them, she just hoped they wouldn't. Lookin' at them they were too good, too beautiful, she didn't deserve them and their daddy didn't want them. Well they were too good for him too. It made you wonder what you did it for. It hadn't been a mistake, she'd wanted the kids, planned them. She just hadn't planned on him not wantin' them an' not sayin'. It all seemed to be about misunderstandings. Not anythin' you meant really. Well it wouldn't change anythin' worryin' about it.

The portrait remained unfinished. Else was quite proud of it really.

Maggi Higgins

In and Out

Jeremy Hughes

"I'm ready", she said.

"Are you sure?"

She nodded and looked at him and put a finger to his lips.

"I'll put things right", he said. He stood up and walked out of the room. She undid the lace collar of her night dress and he returned.

"Help me off with this", she said.

"Don't you want to be covered?"

"No, I'll go naked."

He pulled back the sheets and gently lifted her legs and peeled the nightdress up to her midriff. He did the arms one at a time, then slipped it over her head. She touched her hair into place.

"How do I look?"

"Lovely."

"Lovely," she said to herself, "lovely."

She raised her arms and he bent down, putting his right arm around her back and hooking the left under her knees. He picked her up and walked her out of the room.

The bathroom was large and warm, the walls red. A mirror above the sink was partly obscured by deodorants and sprays. A hairdryer was on the lid of a wicker basket against the bath.

He lowered her into the warm water.

"Wash me."

He took the soap and lathered his hands and smoothed it over her shoulders. He cupped his hands in the water and cleaned her.

"You can go now", she said. "Come back later."

They looked at each other and smiled and kissed.

"Bye, Love", he said.

"Bye."

They kissed again, just pressing their lips against the other's.

He took her hand and they squeezed together, and then he stood up and walked out, closing the door behind him.

She heard the front door go as he went out.

The street was empty. He walked to the newsagents on the corner and bought a newspaper and twenty cigarettes, As soon as he was out of the shop he lit up and deep-breathed the first pull in and out.

The pub was quiet. He went to the bar, got a pint and chased it with a malt. He unfolded the paper along the bar and began reading. He read hard.

"How's the wife?" the barman interrupted.

"She's fine."

"Such a shame."

He nodded and looked at the bubbles rising and glinting in the beer.

The barman sat on a stool at the end of the bar and came across and filled his glass when it was empty.

The pub was dark. Occasionally the sun slanted through the window and lit the pattern in the carpet. A couple came in and sat at a table by a window, their features caught in the light briefly as they leaned towards each other, laughing.

He drank steadily through the afternoon till the sun stopped coming in. His hands were black with print.

Outside, the cold air gave his breathing away and he came into view as he passed below the dim yellow glow of the street lights.

He went in the back door and felt his way across the kitchen to the pantry. He pushed the door open and took a torch off the shelf and switched it on. The electricity meter was turning slowly. He watched the black dot on the disc come round and then he pushed the lever to "OFF".

Corners and objects flitted past his eyes as the torch hit around the rooms. Before he went up the stairs he slipped off his jacket and hung it on the newel post. He took the stairs two at a time.

He pushed the bathroom door and the torch found her hand clutching the hair drier in the water. He put the torch on her face. Her mouth was open.

Jeremy Hughes

Catherine Orr

In Praise of Flat Landscapes

I'll champion flat landscapes
That stretch airy,
Usually to the sea
Rendering perpendiculars
Picturesque.

Kintyre knows them
That plain that rolls
From Crinan, for example;
Druidic playground
Standing stones have room
To stretch their shadows,
A haunted place,
Dunaad's enchanted hillock
Wanders, lost
Within the openness.

I'll champion flat landscapes
That make space for sky,
Endure the wind,
Line-up horizontals
Under sad birds' cries.
Lands of unlocated loss
Gorse, marsh,
And long-backed cattle.

Addressed to the Artist

Daubigny,
I want to bathe in your brush strokes
Immerse myself in that evening calm;
Swim unseeing in the dusk
At one with water
Like otter or seal –
As I have swum in dreams
With no fear.

Daubigny,
Your name is like the water
Stretching, fluid, luminous,
Towards the woods
That wait in silence
To enfold the swimmer
In their soft smudged depths.

House, Harris

Slate and stone and broken glass
Set amid the rock.
Relentless rock,
Scarring, erupting,
Spilling across the hillside –
Slabs, bastions, buttresses
Not craggy, smooth,
The bones of an old land.

Only sheep could pick a living here.
This was never a croft-house
Unless there's a field somewhere, beyond;
And sea, islands, sunsets,
And the time to watch them
Warm the rock.

Slate and stone and broken glass
Deserted not yet derelict.
Others I have seen,
Ruins on lonely hillsides.
I have sojourned in your like
Know the closeness of the stairs,
The narrow landing.
Have wakened to the sound of running feet,
The cries of children.

You cannot endure
Like the indomitable rock
But, slowly, you will settle,
Into a softer mutation.
Raw yet with your own cries
You pose too many questions.

A Musical Request

Oh how we used to sing
Especially in the summer
Washing dishes
In holiday cottages;
Motoring from A to B
Striding, single file
In ankle-scarting heather
Or through the bracken
Waist-high wading,
How we used to sing.

And have the songs grown stale
Sung too often and too long
Or have we lost the zest?
It's hard to force a chorus
Through clenched teeth,
And yet I'm often ambushed by a song
That sings me for hours
Not at my bidding
Nor for a reason
But welling up from
Some subconscious source.

If I could choose
I'd have a song that's overused
Threadbare,
With all the listening
And I'd hear it as I did
The first time
Fresh and new and I
Swamped
By the wonder of it.

Extra-Mural Burrell

Like a primeval tribe,
Hunt-weary,
Threading through the leafless trees
They come to open ground
But know no sense of danger,
Murmuring deep-voiced in the dusk
An easy brotherhood
Strung out on open ground.

The meadow's waterlogged embrace
Clutches heavy-booted feet.
On their breasts the stripes of conflict
Limbs and faces warpaint mud,
From line-out, ruck, and scrum.

How vulnerable they seemed to us
Watching from the wooded path
Bunched above them on the hill.
We could have taken them,
Limb-heavy,
Sluggish on the yielding grass,
Strung-out on open ground.

In lit pavilions through the trees
Worshippers attend their Gods
Stooping, circling, gliding on
In silent, contemplative dance.
Would they have turned
To watch the slaughter
Trapped behind the heavy glass
Aghast among the artefacts.

Catherine Orr

Mórag McCarron

Braes

The wind can't get me here,
I am invisible.
This is a beautiful place,
The streaming grass,
The dry thistle tips.

The gulls are white around boats,
There is a moment dreaming itself
In the whip of wings
And the docile rock is a moment,
Brooding over the water,
Hulking, lost.
Ripped into loneliness.

And what of the clouds washing the sky over?
Sulky, rotund
Brats of the air,
Organs of silence yet
Telling tales of Austria, Japan,
The laden table of the earth,

The earth sends its smells up, tablecloth earth
And I am brainwashed by the clicking of a heron,
Click, click, click, click,
Dreaming of a fish.

The Journey of the Blind Man

How carefully I have compensated;
Erecting pillars with my bare hands.

I have cultivated a plantation of signs;
Your scented voice, my window,
The door where the light rushes,
Gates and latches
The madness of cars.

There is no darkness I fear,
No night that is not my friend,
In this I am stronger than you.

What I fear is the arm that withdraws
Into the textureless void,

The dimming of your laughter.

Origins

I heard the native land was growing in us all;
Sand and daisy coffers, soils sunk from wandering.

I hold on fast, but
Winter chased me off my feet,
Spring beguiled me,
With each Summer came a miraculous fish
While I fished, fished for Autumn
Knowing that here I was already dead.

Then I began to frequent that solemn place;
Memory,
That half-lit, back-street, down-stream place.

Where is your place?
It is hard to say,
Somewhere between the mountains and the plain.
And the sea?
Ahh, the sea...

I was astounded.
I come from the fish.
I am evolved. You too.

So I went to the fishes
Taking bread and great care not to make a sound,
Over the rock pool and the drawbridge moon.

When the nght came, I was far from sleeping.
I heard the creaking of the stars,
The finning of the seas.

And there between kirk and island,
Fishes spawning,
Nets drawing the great ocean.

Fiona Girvan

At Last the Rain

At last the rain,
The precious water my child lacked.

Now,
My womb is empty,
The shadow of death too great to bear,

Oh at last the rain!
The restless water my child lacked
After a season of drought.

To Mircea Eliade

You, small and human as I,
What will you tell me?
Some leaves from your book
Some whisper from your lips.

Your words cross the night:
A thousand times I have heard
These words, insistent as music and
A thousand times I will say
The dream is not yet over.

The deep moon of lost souls is growing,
she is growing and one day
Will vanish,
The white flower of the darkness will vanish
As if gone forever
But the truth is
She is only hidden

And I am already there,
She is full, it is Springtime,
The eyes of the frost open.

The Madman

The language of the madman
Is not on his tongue,

It is buried in his madness.

Someone will tell him
"The garden can cure your ills"
And he'll walk to the sea,
For blades and waves,
Salts and scents
Are all the same in his madness.

The waves will break
"Blossoms", he'll cry,
Gesticulating the sea's heart
With the language of flowers.

But who can speak
Of waves and flowers?

Mórag McCarron

Billy Watt

At the Principal Teachers' Meeting

Sunlight ghosts the unwashed windows
with wintry light. These rows of heads –
sage, cynical, or whatever –
have grown thinner over the years,

and balder too; cut back by nature
as well as fiscal pruning.
So many years, gnawed to the bone
as Hamlet concedes to Polonius...

Sudden clatter of an upturned
OHP as the mutant mental
hero nutters come stampeding
through the door chanting Doc Marten
(PhD) rules OK as they
bovverboot the startled rows run
stamping across the eggboxed heads
headbutt the visiting expert on
flexible learning and then leave
via the tall windows which they
shatter into a Jackson Pollock
splatter of red.

Take that as read,
the Adviser indicates. And now:
How many PTs of English
does it take to change a lightbulb?

Our School (Burnt Down 1991)

Only the rocketing blue
chimney survived, incongruous
as a Victorian promenader

among boiler-house rubble;
around it a scree of slates, torched
like a cancerous house of cards.

All Sunday long parents, children,
stared at gutted ambitions
while local yobs frisbeed plate glass.

The boys who'd doused it in flames,
out of their heads on petrol
or maybe just out of their heads,

would not have seen the papier-mâché
globe that took three Saturday
afternoons and six missed *Neighbours*;

The hamster spinning in its melting
wheel; the jungle of paintings...
all that formed and fixed in the past.

Though maybe they'd written those words
I'd scribbled down five years before:
"God looks like a spike." "He wears clothes

that are too big for him, and sandals."
"God lives in Heaven in his bed."
That stunned morning it was possible

to share in the indifferent
instant before the lobbed bomb,
the nervous giggle at the first kill.

My daughter said, when I asked her:
"It looks like a scary house now.
It looks like it was always like that."

And in its empty space we watched
the blue hills shimmering, fading.

Barbie Dolls on the Bathroom Ledge

A shoe-tree of pink limbs
unfolds on closer inspection

into a collision
of plastic synchronised swimmers.

Impossibly slim arms taper
to palms flattened in royal wave;

their thighs, smooth as wax crayons,
will never whiten slackly in the cold.

Blue eyes form a gaze so direct
you can never meet it. Or hope to.

Breasts are two nipple-less pips
on a conical torso,

the underside of which is smeared
with the merest indentation...

And what of the children
who have discarded these, naked?

They differ by virtue of skin
that puckers with goosebumps, rib-cages

stamped with vulnerability,
eyes that leak Real Tears;

their heads are ill-designed to tilt
upwards with such broken-necked grace.

More than that, their mouths may show
all permutations of pain and joy

but can never match the permanent
bland perfection of these smiles.

Tight
(for Judith)

Into the soft warp of this jumper
for her unborn child, my friend
has knitted a fallen strand of hair.

Though she is young and beautiful
the hair is mottled with grey
like flawed grains in a seam of gold.

As she looks down into herself
in a secret way that she has,
needles focused like waiting beaks,

I am put in mind of Rapunzel
loosing her tenacious curls
into an uncertain future...

and then of the practical woman
who from thick hair of her head
fabricated clothes for three strong sons.

She does not hook the hair out.
Instead her needles tap, dab, tap,
as neat and regular as breaths:

knitting a happy accident
tight into new uncertainty.

Billy Watt

Cemetery Gates

David McVey

Five o'clock; time for Cochrane to shut the gates. The late autumn sun had already gone from all but the highest parts of the cemetery. Cochrane rattled his keys, abandoned his *Daily Record* and the warmth of the hut, and stepped into the sudden chill.

Most days Cochrane would lock the gates and go, but tonight he was in no hurry; the hut was cosy, the radio was particularly good, and he still had the *Evening Times* to read. He locked the gates, giving an involuntary shiver at their metallic coldness, and went back to the hut, anticipating a warm, pleasant hour before the walk home.

He could hear the sound of the radio again when he heard shouts behind him.

"Hoi! Jimmy! Let us oot, will ye?"

There were two men, each carrying a plastic bucket.

"It's much too high tae climb", said one of them.

"All right, all right," said Cochrane, returning to the gate, "but dae ye see that notice? The gates shut at five. Mind that now."

Cochrane made a great fuss of opening the gate, and watched as the men stepped outside. "What's in the buckets?" he asked.

"Brambles", said one, a small weaselly type with gaping teeth which seemed to glow a dull yellow. "Some great bushes up the back there. Show him, Jim."

The other man, dark, sombre, miserable, inclined his bucket so that Cochrane could see inside. It swirled with ripe fruit, which oozed thick red juice, and gave off a sweet, fruity smell.

Cochrane could now remember seeing the men arrive at the cemetery, their hunted air of secrecy, and the three plastic buckets.

"Here, just a meenit", said Cochrane. "There were three of you when you went in. Where's your pal?"

"Who, Dan? He's deid noo, isn't he, Shug?" said Jim.

"Aye, stone deid. Oot like a light. Must have been his hert. He didny even manage tae pick mony berries first."

The men made to leave, but as soon as he was able, Cochrane stopped them with a shouted question. "What are ye sayin -- yer pal dropped deid on the spot, and ye just . . . ye just left him there?"

"Naw, naw", said Jim, in a reassuring tone. "Whit d'ye take us fur? We buried him. There was a hole jist new dug. We used that."

The manner of the two men was casual and diffident, as if they were leaving a betting office, discussing the loss of a couple of pounds.

"But ye cannae do that!" Cochrane persisted, "It's like squatting!"

"Och, don't worry. Ye can always dig anither hole. Dan'll no take up much room. He always kept himself in good shape."

Cochrane was running out of ideas for how to challenge the men, and made one last desperate effort. "What about the burial service? Ye'll no deny yer pal a decent Christian funeral?"

"Dan was an atheist", said Jim.

"Or an agnostic", corrected Shug.

"Naw, naw, definitely an atheist, an a Communist as well. He would've had no time for aa that ashes-to-ashes stuff. When ye're deid, ye're deid, he would say."

In his job, Cochrane was regularly confronted with mortality. Yet as he thought of the man's cooling body, and of the chilly earth which now engulfed it, he was filled with a new dread. It might have been that this unmourned man had never existed.

"What about his family and friends? Ye'll have to tell them."

"He'd nae family. We're his pals. The only wans." Jim thought for a moment, and added, "He'll no be missed."

The cemetery was full, Cochrane realised, of people like Dan. Buried with more ceremony, perhaps, but equally cold, dead and forgotten. Was that all that came after death? Cold, damp earth, and a fading from memory as flesh became dust?

As Cochrane wrestled, he vaguely noticed that Jim and Shug were making no attempt to leave. They stood, nudging each other and whispering, just outside the gates. It was then that Cochrane heard footfalls behind him, and he turned to see a gaunt, grey man in a faded tan raincoat, walking in a leisurely way towards the gates, swinging an empty plastic bucket. He passed through the still-open gates, to join Jim and Shug.

"Here, that's some recovery ye've made, Dan", said Shug.

"It was nae use", said the man. "Efter I tripped doon that hole I tried to gather up aa the berries I dropped, but it was gettin too dark. I'll come again the morra."

As Cochrane mechanically locked the gates, and the men made to walk away, Jim turned and looked apologetically towards Cochrane.

"We had to keep the gates open somehow. There's no way Dan could have sclimmed ower the fence at his age. Ye can see that, eh?"

David McVey

Uncritical Practice?

Graham Dunstan Martin

Are you and I merely a pair of personal pronouns? Have we no individual identity or personal consciousness? The astonishing claim of some deconstructionists is to answer both these questions in the affirmative. For a representative example, Catherine Belsey, in her book *Critical Practice* (Chapter 3, aptly entitled 'Addressing the Subject') attacks the notion of people as subjects, or "autonomous individuals", making reference to the linguistic theories of Emile Benveniste and to theories commonly derived from Ferdinand de Saussure's *Cours de Linguistique Generale* (the famous book put together from Saussure's lectures to his students, following his death in 1913).

According to Benveniste, there is no evidence of subjectivity except our use of personal pronouns when we speak. According to "Saussure", there is nothing positive in language, which is to say there is no positive input from the world into the meanings of language. Only differences *within language* produce meaning. In other words, meaning is created not by the world's nature, but by the languages we speak. Thus the existence of the subject collapses because he is the product of language, and not a natural element in the world's reality.

Having called upon the French psychoanalytic thinker Jacques Lacan to support the drift of this argument, Belsey turns to his Marxist compatriot Louis Althusser and suggests that 'individuals' are constituted by language in the name of ideology. This is why they speak of themselves as acting "freely" and "voluntarily". Such habits are upheld by what Althusser calls "Ideological State Apparatuses", of which the "central" one in contemporary capitalism is the educational system. "It is the role of ideology", Belsey says, "to *construct people as subjects*", quoting Altheusser's 'Ideology and Ideological State Apparatuses' (in *Lenin and Philosophy and Other Essays*; translated from *Positions* (1964-75)). She goes on to claim (p.67) that:

> Capitalism in particular needs subjects who work by themselves, who freely exchange their labour-power for wages... The ideology of liberal humanism assumes a world of non-contradictory...individuals whose unfettered consciousness is the origin of meaning, knowledge and action. It is in the interest of this ideology above all to suppress the role of language in the construction of the subject, and its own role in the interpellation of the subject, and to present the individual as a free, unified, autonomous subjectivity.

She then seeks for something objective as an escape from the subjectivity which is the ironic result of these views.

The difficulty is, of course, that if you assert that no views are freely arrived at, but that all are the result of ideology, then you discount your own view as equally such a result, and no more credible than any other! Belsey is here perilously close to self-explosion, and her way out (pp.63–64) is the following principle: that *inconsistency* shows us untruth. What our ideology tells us about our society is inconsistent, contradictory, non-explanatory. Consequently we may know that our ideology is flawed.

She identifies literary realism as being the liberal humanist celebration of the individual's unbridled freedom. This leads to some discussion of traditional realist literary texts, and to the conclusion that various kinds of modernism are preferable. There is, however, no point in following Belsey onto this terrain, or indeed onto any other, if her initial argument is unsound. On the other hand, if her argument *is* sound, then its consequences are far-reaching – much more radical than the discussion of a few literary texts! What is at stake is nothing less than the status of the human individual.

What is "the liberal humanist ideology"?

We are dealing with an argument that purports to "deconstruct" the subject, as "the origin of meaning, knowledge and action", as possessing "individual freedom, freedom of conscience" and as being "unified and autonomous". We are brainwashed by capitalist society into attributing all of these characteristics to the individual (p.67).

There is a difficulty here: which of the conflicting non-Marxist views of the individual is to be called "liberal humanist"? Freud? Jung? Sartre? Proust? Adam Smith? John Stuart Mill? Aldous Huxley? George Orwell? Hans Küng? Their views are simply not the same at all: for instance the "non-contradictory individual" is quite absent from Proust and Freud. Freedom of conscience and action is not absolute in many systems of thought save perhaps Sartre's; and even there, in the last resort, Sartre's assertion of freedom amounts to no more than the hopeful claim that, even under torture, a victim is still free to keep silent! Nothing unites these thinkers except a negative, namely their non-correspondence with Marxism. Like so many abstract categories, that of "liberal humanism" is empty of content. It is merely a rhetorical device, meaning *all modern thought except Marxist thought*. It is there on Belsey's lips to prevent us seeing the wonderful variousness of human thinking.

Besides, it is arbitrary to assimilate realism to liberal humanism and modernism to socialism as she does. Modernism was banned in most of eastern Europe, under the excuse that it was "decadent individualism". It is the socialist East that developed the theory of "social realism", as is well known. Of course there is still plenty of realism about in the West, but until the socialist East ceased to be socialist it offered nothing *but* realism. Belsey has got this upside down.

Contradictory Subject-Positions

As we saw, Belsey asserts that we can diagnose the falsehood of ideology when it sends us contradictory messages. On p.65 she writes:

> ...women as a group in our society are both produced and inhibited by con-tradictory discourses. Very broadly, they participate both in the liberal humanist discourse of freedom, self-determination and rationality and at the

same time in the specifically feminine discourse offered by society of submission, relative inadequacy and irrational intuition.

That is pretty clear, and I agree with it; but what matters is the conclusions you draw. It appears that Belsey is using it as follows: *Liberal humanist society sends contradictory messages to women. Therefore liberal humanist society is a hypocritical sham. Therefore let us overturn it and replace it with socialism.*

In short, she is misinterpreting active living tensions within society as if they belonged to the quite different category of logical contradictions. The point is that society is not of the same nature as a philosophical argument. A philosophical argument is simply false if it contradicts itself. Society, however, is a complex intermeshing of immense numbers of people with different interests and beliefs. We cannot expect all those interests and beliefs to coincide. The contradictions of society do not disprove its validity (as if society were an abstraction like an argument); rather they show its correspondence to the real variety of the interests of real people within it. A demand that society "cease to be contradictory" amounts to a demand that it suppress variety: a totalitarian demand.

It also presumably allows that society can be self-contradictory *and* real, though apparently the subject *cannot* be real because it is "self-contradictory" (pp 64–65, with reference to Lacan). The subject, we read, is always torn between self and self-image, self-speaker and self-spoken, conscious and unconscious. She assumes that for "subject" to be a coherent notion the subject itself must be coherent. Yet, again, coherence in an argument is one thing, coherence in life quite another. A contradiction in the logic of a sentence is not the same as a tension or conflict in the living of an experience, and it is no objection to the existence of the subject that he or she has contradictory experiences, or that he or she is divided. All natural objects are subdivided, all natural living objects differentiated as to their internal organs, etc. Is it a contradiction that the heart performs one function and the legs another? It is a condition of being alive that one has many different impulses, and that these impulses sometimes clash with one another. This was observed long ago, and is precisely what Greek tragedy is about.

The Subject and Ideology

> I say: the category of the subject is constitutive of all ideology, but at the same time and immediately I add that *the category of the subject is only constitutive of all ideology in so far as all ideology has the function (which defines it) of 'constituting' concrete individuals as subjects.*
> Althusser, quoted by Belsey (p.58)

Let's try and spell that out: it means, "Individuals do not exist. The notion of an 'individual' is a creation of capitalism. And capitalism depends on brainwashing people into thinking themselves individuals". That is very clear, and also perhaps makes clear why Althusser didn't put it that way.

There is, however, at least one subject who remains valid, for he begins with the words "I say". Who is this "I" who, saying that all "I"s are created by capitalist ideology, denies the "I" of individuality? It is Althusser himself. (Though the French text is "*nous ...*", literally "we say", this represents not a statement of a collective point of view but the professorial "*nous*", the regal "we" of authority. This goes unnoticed by Althusser, who belongs to an authoritarian French educational system.)

Why is his view "far-reaching, revolutionary"? Just as our behaviour to the snake we see in the grass will be different if we suppose it to be a dear little rabbit, so our behaviour to our fellow human beings will be different if we suppose them to be artefacts created by social forces rather than autonomous creatures having powers of discrimination and decision. The issues raised are enormous. For one thing, there is the question of the proper relationship between society and the individual (supposing that the latter exists!). If you think that individuals have been manipulated into believing they are individuals, there is no reason why you should not treat them as disposable objects, to be coddled or kicked just as it suits you.

Which seems immediately a good reason for assuming that individuals are real. It is a serious ontological point that the universe seems to consist of nothing but individuals, an individual mouth, individual glass, individual tree, individual paving-stone, individual asteroid. We do not perceive "green-ness" but only green objects. We do not perceive "cruelty" but only cruel actions. Yet we call all mouths mouths, all glasses glasses, and so forth. Our language takes the infinite variety of nature and reduces it to the simplicity of a few general categories. Our language moreover takes the infinite variety of human beings who inhabit this island, and calls them "our society", as if they were the cells in a single jellyfish, or the hardly more independent elements of a parozoon, not the wide variety of complex relationships and relateds that do exist in this seething mass.

Language has to do this, because the complex cannot be handled unless it is simplified. However, Belsey has got the whole problem upside down. Language does *not* promote the idea of the individual, rather it promotes the idea of the category and the collective (the notion that masses of individuals can properly be clumped together under a single collective noun). It is in fact *she* who is at the mercy of the delusive mirages of language. We have spent the whole of history struggling against the generalisations imposed upon us by language, against the delusion that because a man is a "Protestant" you must burn him, or that because a woman is "a woman" she is only fit to sit and sew; the one saving grace in language is the proper name and the personal pronoun, because these alone remind us of the individual reality of things. And here comes Belsey to abolish them!

Ironically, her views would demolish Marxism itself. Marxism came about because Marx saw the working class to be oppressed. The reality of that oppression depended on concrete evidence (or else it would have been merely a piece of metaphysics, or a lie). Suffering cannot be said to happen unless it is *undergone, experienced* or *witnessed* by particular individuals. The whole validity of Marxist protest itself depends on the validity of personal experience. It is only by making space for personal experience that one can make space for moral argument.

Belsey's assault on the individual, and hence on personal experience, is particularly radical. She asks: Would subjects be thought to exist at all if it were not for language? The mind boggles. *A world without subjects?* What is the alternative to a world of subjects? The clear implication is that an Althusserian state would abolish personal pronouns outright.

Is the subject created by language?

On p.59 of Belsey we find the following quotation from Benveniste:

> ...The basis of subjectivity is the exercise of language. If one really thinks about it, one will see that there is no other objective testimony to the identitiy of the subject except that which he himself thus gives about himself.
> (*Problems in General Linguistics*, Miami, 1971, p.226)

Really? Is it solely because you say "I" of yourself that I suppose you to be "you"? Is language so omnipotent? Has it that infinite power of creation which was traditionally attributed to God? Benveniste is making an elementary mistake. Take the case of a deaf-mute, say Helen Keller: is he suggesting, monstrously, that Helen Keller wasn't conscious before she learnt to speak? In *The Story of My Life* she notes that she did use a deficient and self-invented sign language before she found her teacher, and that language was a joyous "release from prison". To be released from prison, however, one has to be a prisoner; and to be a prisoner one has to *be*.

Come to that, because he doesn't talk English, or Manx or even Siamese, does my cat have no identity? Is he not a subject, or a subjectivity, whatever these terms may be supposed to mean? Is the minimum conceivable explanation of his behaviour not that (a) he feels painful and pleasurable sensations, (b) has desires and drives, (c) doesn't question his remaining as an identity through time, (d) has a sense of possession of territory, including the possession of (we would say "by") his owners, and (e) has little use for ideology?

Is Belsey right about Benveniste? She quotes him (p.59):

> Language is possible only because each speaker sets himself up as a subject by referring to himself as 'I' in his discourse.

But if language *depends* upon the notion of subjective identity, then it is clear that the notion of subjective identity, being the precondition of language, comes *before* language. Moreover, Benveniste explains in his *Problèmes de Linguistique Generale* (tome 1, Paris, 1966, p.227) that there is no known language in which distinctions of person, attached to the verb, are not marked in some way or other. The reasonable assumption to make is that, since no language exists without personal subjects, then those personal subjects are a necessary part of the environment within which language grows.

The contradictions here are too great to overlook. Benveniste's words in French are:

Si l'on veut bien y réfléchir, on verra qu'il n'y a pas d'autre témoinage objectif de l'identité du sujet que celui qu'il donne ainsi lui-même sur lui-même (ibid, p.262).

How different it sounds in French! Is this not a case of that common French figure of speech, hyperbole? Benveniste is not asserting the truth of his statement, but merely underlining it. Due to the work of our old friend Doctor Rhetoric, Benveniste has been misunderstood.

According to Benveniste and Saussure, writes Belsey (p.59), "it is language itself which, by differentiating between concepts, offers the possibility of meaning." In other words, before language comes along there are no meanings.

Flattering as this may be to the human animal, it is quite clear that the rest of the animal kingdom, despite its lack of words, can perfectly well distinguish between one thing and another. Wolves can tell a chipmunk from a tree, rabbits know their mates and recognise their predators, whether swooping from above or charging through bushes. Such distinctions are nothing less than the condition of survival itself. Thus, when Belsey writes (p.61) that "it follows from Saussure's theory of language as a system of differences that the world is intelligible only through discourse", she is in manifest error. It follows from the behaviour of 'dumb' animals that differences are distinguishable to the senses well before language emerges, and have been from near the beginning of life on this planet. What does anyone suppose the senses to be but a system which enables animals to distinguish between hot and cold, friend and foe, meat and mate? The senses can be viewed as an internalised sign-system. The whole theory of semiotics is in fact posited on the principle that language is not the only sign-system. As sign-systems go, it is one of the latest to appear on the scene.

In any case, how did language ever come about? The answer must be, (a) it must have a ground to stand on, but also (b) it must alter that ground in a useful fashion. For otherwise *there would be no reason for it to appear.* This in turn means that there must be a ground, because, if there were no ground, what would be the point of altering or manipulating it?

The internal sensory sign-systems of animals set up systems of difference hundreds of millions of years before language appeared. It is generally held, by scientists as by ordinary people in the ordinary business of life, that these differences within the sign-systems reflect to some degree and with some allowance for error, differences in the outside world. Did Saussure really disagree? Suppose he does, ought he to? As one writer observes:

> ... one may give a sociological account of why we come to make the dis-
> tinctions we do; but there must be something about the world which makes
> these distinctions possible. *That* we distinguish between cats and dogs may
> be due to certain social conditions; that we *can* so distinguish has something
> to do with cats and dogs. (Richard Pring, 'Knowledge out of Control',
> *Education for Today*, Autumn 1972, p 25).

This is obviously true. Why, then, did Saussure disagree with it? As noted above, Saussure sleeps secure in the arms of uncertainty: his book was not written by himself but reconstructed by students.

Never mind whether Saussure's view is correctly described by Belsey. If the notions of "I", "you" and "she" are the product of the difference-making nature of language, and if there are no differences in nature, but these are merely imposed on language, then "I", "you" and "he" are merely the product of language and not of reality. Thus the subject finds himself or herself totally abolished. S/he is an illusion imposed on us by the languages we speak. S/he is an accidental figment of grammar (or accidence, as it used to be called).

Let us see what this implies. If the argument is correct, it is not merely the subject who can produce no evidence for his/her own evidence save that of language. The same is true of cats, spiders, plagues, AIDS, deaf-aids, President Bush's aides, socialists called Gorbachev, rainbows, bikinis, the difference between girls and boys, saying hurrah about that: in short, everything.

The argument used by Belsey to reduce the person to a mere accident of accidence, reduces all other notions to equal linguistic arbitrariness. In consequence, it rebounds upon itself. The subject remains just as true as, and no more false than, any other supposed real entity. He or she remains as true or as false as the skyscraper in the square, the baby in the cot and the Boeing in the sky.

As her claim thus collapses, let us just lean back and admire the enormity of it. Language is in this view of things the Almighty, because by creating difference it quite simply creates – out of the inscrutable, indecipherable confusion of the world – *everything*. Here is a new Absolute, dragged in through the back door on the authority of the prophet Saussure and some others. This smacks of Tibetan prayer-wheels and charms against warts. If language can create reality, why don't we sometimes *catch it* doing just that?

Contradictions of Deconstruction

Let me at this point draw into the argument the high priest of Deconstruction, Derrida himself. If I read his theory and practice aright, any act of discourse can be deconstructed, including the act of deconstruction. One might expect such acts of reiterated deconstruction to successively reinstate and then deconstruct the subject once more. The subject would successively disappear and reappear. Thus the technique could not disprove the existence of the subject.

In Belsey's own text, language about ideology and "society" is always strongly personified. Thus she writes: "Ideology *suppresses* the role of language in the construction of the subject" (p.61, my italics). It "appears to provide answers", it "masquerades" (pp.57, 104). Renaissance science "initiated a process" etc., from which Christianity "has never recovered" (p.130). Intentional, independent activity has been displaced from the individual and relocated in the abstraction and in the collective. Similarly, the author's independent activity has been removed from him, and relocated in the text. It "enlists the reader" (p.103) and "implicitly criticises its own ideology" (p.109); and she writes of "the unconscious of the text" (p.107). Admittedly this tendency to personification is unavoidable, because it is impossible to visualise a language devoid of verbs which imply intentional activity. But if we may deconstruct the individual subject, and move his intentional activity into the collective, there is no reason why we should not deconstruct the collective and move its allegedly intentional activity back into the subject.

Nor is it clear, according to the practice of deconstruction, how we might prove one of these positions to be preferable to the other. For Derrida casts doubt upon the notion of proof by suggesting that the posing of a question always predetermines the outcome of the investigation that follows. Belsey's whole project is therefore undermined from the outset if we apply to it the principles of Derrida. Although that project is no more undermined than any other project would be, it is only to be concluded that she has not deconstructed the subject, which remains hale and hearty despite her efforts. This is not surprising: how can an argument disprove the existence of the very thing which proved the argument? All arguments depend ultimately on conscious perceptions and thus no argument can disprove conscious perceptions without disproving itself. Thus, Democritus showed the intellect as saying,

Only ostensibly is there colour, sweetness, bitterness; actually only atoms and void.

But the senses reply:

"Poor deluded intellect! You get your evidence from us, and you hope to overthrow us? Your victory is your defeat!"
(Democritus of Abdera, *Diels*, frg. 125)

It follows that, since (as far as anyone knows) no conscious perceptions occur, save as perceived by individual consciousnesses, no argument can disqualify individual consciousnesses without disqualifying itself.

Moreover, there are at least two kinds of act – the act of the rational type and the act of the volitional type. The former is in practice dependent on the latter, for no one performs the rational act without wishing to do so. But a wish presupposes a why. Why should anyone want to have no subjects? So as to have no one to resist the collective? If that is so, then the subject would indeed become a subject (i.e. helplessly subjected to political power), which is precisely the play of words Belsey quotes (p62) from Althusser, but with an opposite intention. Her desire corresponds with his: to suggest that it is "free subjects" who are, unknown to themselves, slaves.

But how can it assist those "slaves" to tell them that not only are they not free subjects, but that there is no such thing as a subject, free or not? We are alarmingly close to the languge of Orwell's *1984*, where "freedom is slavery" and persons can become "unpersons". Althusser's play on words is deadly.

Nor is it possible to overlook the fact that deconstruction is an act performed by subjects. If you ask me "How do we know that it is not an act performed by society *through* subjects?" I should reply that no one has ever seen society speaking except through the mouths of individuals. Society is dumb, it has no voice, it cannot hold a pen, and therefore only a subject could persuade me that he is not a subject. I should also say, "The form of your sentence is most peculiar for someone who disbelieves in subjects. Who are these personal pronouns you mention when you say, '*we know*'?" For how are issues decided save by subjects? Surely that is what "deciding an issue" means? Or do you want to revert to deciding questions by authority? Aren't those who assert authority subjects too?

It does, however, seem presumptuous of this deconstructionist to tell the rest of us that we don't exist. Even her implied claim that she doesn't exist either looks like a lame excuse in the light of such an act of self-aggrandisement

Graham Dunstan Martin

I fought in the war, ken!

Alexander Innes

"I's top-heavy," said McTaggart, "I's top-heavy."

"What is?" asked the stranger.

"Ma heid," said McTaggart, with the utmost sincerity, "Ma heid."

The stranger looked puzzled for McTaggart's head did not appear in the least top-heavy to him, in fact it looked altogether quite normal.

"Why, or rather how, is it top-heavy?" he asked.

"I's full o shrapnel!" said McTaggart, and gave a self-satisfied nod, with his lips pursed and the slightest hint of a world-weary shake of his head. "Fu' o shrapnel."

McTaggart was a small, round-shouldered man, with a knack of only looking you in the eye when he wanted a drink. He wore an old gaberdine raincoat that had seen several too many spillages, and a football scarf long since disowned by its team. He stared at his shoes, scuffed and scarred by a thousand kerbstones and murmured about shrapnel.

"I fought in the war, ken", he said finally. "I wis a Desert Rat."

For a moment he stood, or seemed to stand erect and tall, with a hint of pride in the eye which looked steadily into the stranger's.

"A Desert Rat, in the war, ken?"

He was in danger of faltering, for the stranger was not responding, only staring back at him, meeting his gaze with incomprehension. McTaggart was used to rejection but not to this; his gaze was beginning to weaken, to lose the stranger's eye. "The war, ken?" he said helplessly.

"The war, yes, really", said the stranger finally. "Did you now?"

He was feeling almost as awkward as McTaggart and knew what his only escape could be.

"Ah, will you have a pint?" he asked, reaching quickly inside his overcoat for his wallet.

McTaggart's eyes flicked from the stranger's old school tie back to his eyes, then shied away from their desperation and pity.

"Aye, sure son, sure, a pint'll be fine, be fine."

He pushed his hand into his coat pocket and wrenched it out again, then kicked a cigarette-end across the floor.

"Just fine", he said again, but the stranger had turned towards the bar. McTaggart looked around the bar to see if anyone had seen his latest shame, but their faces were buried in their papers or their beers, or turned skyward towards the television's warm glow.

"A Desert Rat, eh? My old dad was with the Eighth Army too", said the stranger, handing McTaggart a dripping glass of beer. "Perhaps you came across each other out there in the desert?"

For a moment McTaggart felt the old familiar panic rise in him, but he had been through this before and knew how to behave.

"S'at right," he said, his mouth in the foam of his beer, "is it?"

"Yes," said the stranger, "he was a captain of infantry."

The phrase struck him immediately as being pompous and somehow Napoleonic, and he regretted it. To McTaggart, however, it was a lifeline.

"I was in tanks masel", he rushed out. "They aye pit wee boys like me intae tanks, dinnae tak up sae much room, see. No sae much room."

"Right, right", the stranger nodded, relieved that this poor little figure had not picked up his pompous figure of speech.

"What were you then? Driver? Gunner? Loader?"

McTaggart felt the panic again. Did this bloke know anything about tanks, and would he pick him up on a slip? He buried his mouth in the foam again, and taking what sounded like the easiest option, said "Loader, I wis a loader."

"God," said the stranger, "that must have been hellish, the heat, the confined space, the noise, the smell of cordite and, and everything really..." His voice trailed off into a question-mark.

"Aye", said McTaggart, who did know about hot, sweaty, noisy, confined spaces with hardly any light to see by and the threat of disaster only a thought away.

"It wis that. It wis hellish, that's what it wis. Hellish."

He shook his head fiercely as if to rid himself of the memory of hell itself, and looked the stranger straight in the eye.

"Hellish." He put his empty glass on the counter.

The clunk of glass on wood startled them both and sent the stranger's glass to his mouth in an involuntary arc. He was now feeling trapped and embarrassed. Here he was standing at the counter of a grubby little backstreet bar, rushing a pint of beer and being transfixed by an equally grubby little ex-soldier as if he were a rabbit caught in headlights. It was ridiculous, but he was powerless to escape from the developing situation. He knew, just as McTaggart knew, that he was going to buy him another pint; it was unavoidable, ineevitable, and he felt somehow ashamed.

"Another pint?" he asked, wrenching himself away from the gaze.

"Aye, thanks son. Thanks. Much appreciated." McTaggart seemed to sense the tension of embarrassment and felt that he had to do something to defuse the situation. He was onto a good thing. He knew it, and he did not want to lose it. As the stranger handed him his second pint, he ventured "Eh, what d'ye dae yersel, like?"

"Me? Oh, I'm a chartered accountant", said the stranger.

"That must be interesting", ventured McTaggart, striking out into uncharted waters. He took a generous swallow from his pint and waited for the reply, but the stranger was looking at the floor and did not speak. "Accountancy", prompted McTaggart, "must be interesting."

But the stranger was drawn to the idea of the little Desert Rat, although he did not know why he should be. He could only think about this small, semi-literate figure cramped into a steel death-trap, sweating fear and blood in the same western desert which had scarred his own father for what was the rest of his life.

"So how was it in the tanks, then, in battle?" he asked, not fully understanding why he persisted.

McTaggart was taken aback, not knowing if the stranger had twigged and was taking the piss, or if he was serious and really interested.

"It was hellish", he said.

"Were you afraid?"

"Aw aye, terrified, maist o the time, aye." McTaggart was fighting his own desperate rearguard action now, feeling the panic well up inside him again. "Terrified", he said. The way the stranger looked at him McTaggart knew he would have to say more, that he would have to share his old fears. It was the only way out for him now, the only way.

"Ye're all cooped up, right? You can hardly move or breathe; there's sweat everywhere. In yer eyes, runnin doon yer erms an legs. Yer ba's itch an ye cannae scratch, an aa the time there's the noise, an the dust, the choking dust, an the smell, an, an yer jist bangin away, waitin fir it tae end wan way or the other at any minnit. It's... it's fuckin hellish!" McTaggart stopped. He had started to sweat. He didn't really know where it had all come from, but as he grasped his drink and gasped it down he felt a feeling he only half-understood begin to surface from somewhere in his mind.

"Sorry, son, sorry about that, I... I jist needed to get it out."

He ducked his head toward his scuffed feet and his mismatched shoelaces and sighed.

"That's all right", said the stranger, shocked and taken aback by the outburst, feeling ashamed for putting the old man through it. He responded in the only way he could think of. "Another drink? A nip, maybe?"

McTaggart was too wrapped up in his own thoughts to look up, and just nodded. The stranger turned to the barman, who had been watching the whole scene with detached interest. He had never seen McTaggart give a better performance, and he had seen them all.

"A pint and a whisky, please", the stranger asked.

"A double is it?" replied the barman. After all that, he felt McTaggart deserved a double.

"Yes, a double, thank you." The stranger avoided the barman's eyes and reached inside his overcoat for his wallet. He glanced at McTaggart, who was finishing his drink. He watched as the old man laid the empty glass on the counter and licked his lips. He looked at the shabby figure half-cowered against the bar counter and could not help but see him as he must have been, eyes wide with terror, crouched over a burning hot gun breach – his mouth full of his own sweat, and the taste of his fear.

The stranger pocketed the change and handed the two drinks to McTaggart, who nodded his thanks, but still the stranger was driven to know more. He couldn't help it. It was not simply the fascination, morbid or otherwise, that he felt for McTaggart and his past: somehow this little man held some sort of key to his understanding of the horror of his own father's experiences. He had to know more.

"And the shrapnel?" he asked, haltingly.

"Oh Christ, will it never end?" thought McTaggart, who had hoped that he was finally off the hook. The panic rose once again as McTaggart attempted to compose himself, his mind racing to find an answer that would rid him of his tormentor. He slowly raised his hand from the depths of his panic and looked the stranger full in the eyes.

"We got hit", he said. "Got hit."

"yes, yes of course you did, of course you did", the stranger said, suddenly aware that he had gone too far, and suddenly all too aware of what he had said and done.

"I'm sorry," he said, "I'm sorry."

"Ye dinnae huv tae be sorry, son", said McTaggart, who realised that he was in control of the situation. "It was a long, long time ago."

They looked at each other for a few moments, then the stranger looked away.

"Look, I have to go", he said. "I only really stopped by for a quick pint. I've… I've enjoyed talking to you, but I'll have to go." He felt now as if he were standing before his father, a boy again, having been ticked off for his behaviour and desperate to leave, but unable to move until he was told to go. "I'll have to go. Sorry", he said.

McTaggart looked at him steadily for a moment longer, then said "That's okay, son, I understand. Thanks for the drinks, very kind o ye, very kind." He turned away and bowed his head slightly over the bar, one hand cupped around his whisky glass, now deep in his own thoughts and memories.

The stranger shuffled uneasily, then turned and walked towards the door, but at the end of the bar the barman stopped him.

"Look, pal, wee Mac's guid an he's no such a bad boy really, but I think there's somethin you should know. I mean, he's no exactly everythin he says he is or was, ken?"

"That's okay," said the stranger, "I don't want to know."

"But back in the war, men like him didnae huv tae go tae…"

The stranger interrupted him. "It's okay. I said that I didn't want to know. I don't want to be told. It's okay!" The stranger heard his voice rise and drew a deep breath. "I must go. Thank you anyway. It's okay, honestly." He buttoned his overcoat and looked down the length of the bar to where McTaggart stood, crumpled in his gaberdine. "Good night", he said. The barman shuffled back. "Suit yersel, pal, I jist thought…"

The stranger shook his head and smiled, partly at his own predicament, and partly at the old man hunched over the counter rubbing his hands together. He gave McTaggart a last look then turned and left the bar.

McTaggart, meanwhile, stood in silence, staring into the depths of his whisky, wondering where his next one would come from, rubbing his hands, feeling each and every callous and scar earned in a lifetime spent working underground in the hot, noisy, confined spaces of the pit. As his fingers interwined he remembered his blind, despairing terror when the roof collapsed and it seemed to take a lifetime to dig him out, and how afterwards any sound would make that fear rise in him again. He remembered *his* war, the one that hadn't finished in 1945 but had lasted every day until he retired.

"Some reserved occupation", he muttered, half to himself.

Alexander Innes

Norman Gariock

Distractions

i

This rock that falls and falls through silence
survived the ascent of man and, spinning
in endless imagining, hardly troubles
the stream of time; three stones from the sun,
here I stand on a summer morning, alone.
From a small-town treeless island home
I came to this place among poplars and elms
where a starling's ecstatic skein of song
celebrates all time past, all time to come
in its verdant cathedral at dawn.
Keats and Shelley knew this sensation,
the sacred promise behind all religion;
standing here I might almost believe in
a creation beyond the assault of mind.

ii

The sun blinks green-bright across the ocean's
grand arc, rises clear over Autumn fields
and sweeps blue shadows off country lanes.
Like chased copper on burnished gold
The horses wait. Cattle, fully rounded
against a hasty sketch of sky, feign
disinterest with a slow rotation
of heavy jaws. A motor starts. The road,
like a cancel-line across a page, transects
the scene; there is no wilderness we can
not tame. A discarded fridge glints, reflects
the distant conurbation and shows
a cartographic grid of shadows
in a jewelled icon of flaking chrome.

iii

A light coughs on bright and raw in an upstairs
room, burning like a sore till the spasm subsides.
A woman appears. Feline and sleek, her feet
prod knowingly amongst the excrement
and the garbage. Symbolic stars, reflected
in puddles, wink out to silk and suspenders
as she passes. Some where a baby cries,

then stops. And the neon Church's noise repeats
crippled music to the empty streets; selected
Mozart with a four-four beat ferments.
And the icons fall in slo-mo relief
on fading film in the media glare;
and sucking crumbs from between rotting teeth
I long out past roofs to the forest there.

iv

Mute in the shade of this vespertine arch
I exalt in the void, our ancient bequest;
the forest's enclosured compassing church
amplifies the silent palimpsest.
Here, realith implies its extensions
and past mid present melds. But still I shrink
in awed retreat under civilisation's
paternal slow blink, denying instinct.
Ideas converge, light in a prism;
conflagration igintes in burnished choirs.
No carolings call, but silence; optimism
empties under dim lit lichened spires.
And the sun comes up and the traffic
and the shadows sheen tenebrific.

December Day; Hoy Sound

Tall as a plough-team, archetypal silence
waits, denying the maelstrom rains' advance.

But black-starred against our low horizon,
the children play at soldiers, American;
second-hand adults with imported clothes on,
drawling their accents to legato drones.

Me as I was, and will be, now smiled upon
by tourists and exiles glad of the familiar;
comforted here by the distorted patois
of a self-conscious welcome, home from home.

Fret-worked by tides, loch blotched and foreign,
our landscape is shaped with filters for fantasy;
the Fable, re-invented by industry
as mares-tails whip, fast shadow the sun.

And those shadows hurl across every scene
and the grasslands rage like fire-fanned wind
behind impossible tons at the speed of sound.
The Horses are gone; Muir's Eden, fallen.

Graffiti

Just recognisable for what they are, these
vague shapes in the soil must fascinate us.
It's like coming across an old school jotter
and recognising your own name, mis-spelt
and crudely drawn, on the yellowing paper;
even after years those letters can be felt
raised on the backs of the pages like braille.
It's the same with these ruins, despite the years
their shapes remain as legible as that scrawl.
Written in stone, these circles and squares
punctuate the diary of our struggle.
"I was here" are the words we can trace,
written repeatedly in such feeble
scratchings across every vacant surface.

Norman Gariock

Ruth Thomas

Highland Hispanic Taurus

Being a big, black bull with pointed horns
And fashionable nose-ring,
I'm none too keen on the colour of your car.
Why did you choose that goading red to
Roam my island in?

I'll stand in your way, plant my hooves
On the muddy track and dare you
To edge one inch past.
The only red that I respect is on
The backs of brothers

Whom I'll not brawl with, only you –
If you'd leave your car I'd let you go
But red reveals that you're no more
Than a tourist toreador.

Washing Day

In the silver-plated kitchen
Washing struggles
Like the arms of angry men
Jousting for chalices of water.

Next door is cool
And jungle-lined with plants.
Two kittens gnaw at papers, then start
Softer wars on curtains and old corks.

I sit. Day greys.
The sky is carved with chimney-pots
And laced with scaffold.
Men trumpet from the planks,

Their brains the size of buttons
Or a quickly waning moon –
That pale gleam like rounding
Pods of honesty,

Stuck brittle into vases,
Washed dry like the midnight tights
I drag out of the opened mouth.

Porridge

Porridge is a pauper's solace,
Oaten soup good for the body
Made with water, grit with salt;
Good for the soul made with milk,
Laced with sugar.

Porridge is an island in a sea of milk.
Sugar is a forest, the spoon is a plane.
That is what the children learn before
They learn to like it.
That is what they will recall in sager,
Lumpen years.

Mrs Quill Overhears

Late afternoon, and Mrs Quill
Drinks tea from café cups.
Tucked snug behind a table
She spears chat like a pirate
Slicing seed cake.

Under a charming clock she hears
Three woollen ladies dissect an
Old friend. 'My dear, she's
Run off with another man –
Calls it recycling...'

The café's filled with brass and
Dead flowers and, ill-timed, a head,
Dismembered, shines whitely through
High panes of glass; it smiles to see
Its three old friends

Whose voices sink and drown in waves
Of scalding and embarrassed tea.
Beneath the seed crumbs Mrs Quill
Hides evidence as the elderly exit,
Stabbing a last image of the rouge
That sticks their faces on.

What She Does

Slides the switch. Sticks Groove Holmes over
The silver spike, drinks tea. Misses him.

Feed the cats with insufficients. Yes,
The rain is like a tilted ocean

But still she'll steer the Good Ship Red Umbrella
Towards that distant shore, Provisions.

Sailing home she has to turn her collar up.

Mid-morning, time to lie on her stomach, swing
Her legs, listen to that shuffle on the record

Like an egg-whisk on a dustbin lid.

And tonight's the night for bins and Board Meeting.
Still not condensing those words enough;

She'll never learn to turn Discussion to
"This was discussed".

Has a piss. Puts on a puckered coat. Leaves
the red umbrella dripping on the kitchen floor.

Misses him.

Ruth Thomas

AGENDA

TOM SCOTT SPECIAL ISSUE

Contributors include Kathleen Raine, Alan Bold,
Tom Hubbard, William Neill, W S Milne, Peter
Russell, Thom Nairn, Carla Sassi, Robert Calder

Price £8

Agenda, 5 Cranbourne Court, Albert Bridge Road, London SW11 4PE

Tom Scott *The Collected Shorter Poems*

Coming soon, a joint *Agenda/Chapman* production

including Brand the Builder, The Ship, The Paschal Candill and
many other well-known poems

£11.95 from Agenda or Chapman

Language, Race, Nation and Gender
a Post-colonial Meditation

Shirley Geok-lin Lim

In the US Academy, the axiom that knowledge is power, which has been read conventionally as a race- and gender-free proposition, is almost always applied differently to non-European Americans and to women scholars. Werner Sollars has argued (in *Beyond Ethnicity: Consent and Descent in American Culture*, New York, OUP, 1986), through an examination of selected American literary texts, that the construction of American identity proceeds by way of consent, with the individual abandoning a pre-immigrant culture and voluntarily accepting modes of behaviour and systems of belief associated with American culture. Consent as the predominant paradigm of Americanisation counters the descent paradigm, in which identity remains embedded in genealogical blood-lines, and the individual is constrained in construction of identity to some essentialist notion of birth-affect and tribal influence. Sollors' reading of the consent-descent dichotomy of ethnic identity formulation is appealing precisely because it appears to support the ideological matrix of democratic individualism that is usually presented as 'the American Way'. His consent theory to explain the relatively smooth process of assimilation by European immigrants into the American social mainstream, however, overlooks how the descent paradigm operates differently for people of colour (that is, all distinctively non-European-looking Americans).

Let us take the problem of language requirement in one area of the knowledge industry. In the field of American literature, scholars are still expected to have a reading knowledge of at least two other languages than English. In the sub-field of Asian-American literature, more and more the expectation is that the scholar should have at least one major Asian language in hand. As Asian-American literature is to a large extent written in English by writers who are themselves unable to write in the language of their Asian ancestors, this expectation points to an unacknowledged emphasis on descent. The racial origin of the producer, validated by the possession of a "descent" language, is presented as having a significant bearing on the reproduction of knowledge in that particular subset. Thus, in treating American ethnic literature, the racial identity of the interlocutor is valorised as a significant signature, assigning authority, authenticity and validity to his/her reading. The same kind of descent association is not made of mainstream American critics: for example, Lionel Trilling's Jewish identity does not prevent him discussing Anglo-American writing, nor does one ask that a critic be versed in Armenian or Yiddish to appreciate William Saroyan's or Bernard Malamud's works.

Colonial and post-colonial non-consent

This ascription of authority to descent does not take into account the diachronic and provisional dimension of language/knowledge acquirement (as in the question of language acquirement in a recent past, for example the colonised world of Malaysia), but reads discourse in the synchronicity of the contemporary. The critique of colonised cultures is well-rehearsed by writers such as Franz Fanon, Memmi, and Chinweizu[1]. Post-independence, the sociopolitical model of an anomic, alienated, English-speaking native intelligensia-élite produced by a British Imperial administration is accepted in these critiques as replicable whether in Trinidad, Singapore, Ghana, Kenya or India. In both colonial and post-colonial constructions of the intelligensia-élite and the relation of language choice to its construction, however, the crucial factor of consent is overlooked. The colonial government, in setting up English-language schools and a system of civil service rewards based on English-language acquirement, did not require the consent of the populace.

Similarly, from 1970, in dismantling that English-language educational and civil service structure, and in establishing a native-language-base power-structure, the Malay-dominant government in Malaysia did not ask for the consent of its non-Malay citizens. In colonial and post-colonial societies, language policies took effect, whether to the empowerment or displacement of the English language, de facto, outside the area of democratic discussion and decision. The bias remains that individuals do not so much choose a language of affiliation or have that choice politically foisted upon them as that the choice has always already been made through the essential bond of race and blood-line.

The Chinese-Malaysian and language choice

What seems to be a straightforward proposition of identifying language with the people, "the folk", can be seen as problematic in post-colonial societies. In a nation like Malaysia nothing can be taken for granted in examining the relationship between the individual's localised speech-world and national language culture. Chinese Malaysians, for example, would be expected to feel an affiliation for Bahasa Malaysia, the national language. Embracing place as origin, the Chinese Malaysian may adopt the national language in an assimilative act similar to the Nonyas and Babas of the Straits Settlements. However, if Bahasa is seen as an instrument of empowering one racial group and consequently of disempowering the Chinese Malaysians, the language itself may rouse strong feelings of disaffiliation, and be used only when necessary. The same Chinese Malaysian may turn to the language of descent to express resistance to a national formation that appears to erase his or her identity. The language of race may be Mandarin, the élite Chinese of writing and communication. Or, having lost any sense of affiliation with the Chinese of origin, the Chinese Malaysian may simply continue to use dialect, asserting a local Chinese, as opposed to national Chinese, identity. Or Chinese Malaysians,

1. Franz Fanon, *Black Skins, White Masks*, trans Charles Lam Markmann (New York, Grove, 1967); Albert Memmi, *The Colonizer and the Colonized*, trans Howard Greenfeld (New York, Orion, 1965); Chinweizu et al, *Decolonising the African Mind* (Lagos, Pero, 1987).

rejecting both Malay and Chinese cultural nationalisms, both based on paradigms of racial descent, assent to an international language that opens the future for themselves and their children, English. These Malaysians, in choosing the future over the past, consent over descent, are choosing a potential international identity formulation over national identity-politics deformation which reinscribes ancient tribal feuds and territorial imperatives. They are choosing the potential open border of immigration over the already closed boundary of the nation-state.

Exiles, refugees, and immigrants

In a post-colonial world, where exiles, refugees and immigrants form the majority of its citizenry, language-choice must increasingly be dissociated from racial origin and possession, a matter of descent, and become increasingly associated with matters of economic, political and material circumstances. Language choice and possession are less an unproblematic voice of a people, a marker of tribalised identity, a mythologised origin, an idealised notion of racial purity and authenticity, reified in time, changeless, than problematised products of economic forces that include the movements of peoples globally in response to capitalist labour demands, the resistance of indigenous ideologies forming around similar notions of unalienated labour and capital supply, and so forth.

The Little Tree controversy

Let us return to the expectation that a scholar of Asian-American literature should possess one major Asian language. This Asian language requirement is provocative for more reasons than those of disagreements concerning professional certification. At the heart of the provocation is the unspoken issue, who speaks for whom? And behind that the more difficult question, what qualifies the speaker? There may be little disagreement when one operates in the clearly-defined areas of political representation. An elected spokesperson is validated by the votes of the majority to speak for his/her electorate. But in the issue of minority or ethnic literary production, complicated issues are raised as to who is qualified to write, for example, of the Native American experience.

The question of author's identity is no easy matter of essentialist false-reasoning or red-herring "authenticity" debates in the example of *The Education of Little Tree* (Forrest Carter, *The Education of Little Tree*, University of New Mexico Press, 1990). An uplifting, politically-correct tale narrating the experiences of a young Native American, it sold as a best-seller until it was discovered that the author was a white American racist who had written speeches for the Ku Klux Klan. This "discovery" of white racism in the author immediately casts doubt on the "sincerity" if not authenticity of the text, reminding us that literary texts as social products are therefore open to such social questions as sincerity and authenticity. Literature can no longer be hidden behind, protected by an argument of its sacral textuality: it is exposed as vulnerable, as we human cultural producers and reproducers are, to social, political and economic contingencies and critiques.

Does the author's racism change the nature of the text of *The Education of Little Tree*? This question cannot be put aside easily. The signature (source of authority) must necessarily taint the text, for a white racist, one may reasonably suspect, may not fully believe in what the text purports to demonstrate. The relation between a fiction and the imagination that produces it is not unsubstantial. A reader forearmed with the knowledge of Little Tree's non-Native American white supremacist past begins to read the text in a different context, one of hidden racist or racialist signs, of duplicity, manipulativeness; an artifice significantly, politically removed from the artifice of fiction. Who is doing the speaking is as significant in affecting the ways we decode that language as what language the author chooses to speak in.

Feminist criticism: the signature of the woman

In such an ethnic-marked situation, racial identity is a factor in influencing and guiding interpretation. The emphasis on identity is also marked in much of US feminist criticism. In an odd conjunction of theoretical concerns, the most positivist and materialist of feminist critics in the US, women usually concerned with political and economic analysis for specific corrective social agendas, agree with a number of French feminist theoreticians that the identity of the speaker is crucially related to the nature of the language deployed. Nancy Miller, a US-based French literature critic, argues that authorship is a complex "contextual activity" that involves agency and shows the "marks of a producing Subject" (Nancy K Miller, *Subject to Change: Reading Feminist Writing*, New York, Columbia University Press, 1988, p18). It is important that we maintain the signature of the woman writer for political reasons, as this woman's signature leads to "resistance to dominant ideologies (and) is the site of a possible political disruption". In looking at language, we must continue to emphasise the gender identity of the producer, the "feminine" tradition that the text contributes to and that forms the context by which the text is to be politically understood. For Miller, in reading a woman's text, we undertake "a double (intertextual) reading – of the autobiography with the fiction" as a way of "deciphering a female self".

French feminists work against the usual feminist critique of language as a phallocentric-because-logocentric institution: Helene Cixous and Luce Irigaray argue that this phallocentricity can be transformed by woman's language: "Because the oeconomy of [woman's] drives is prodigious, she cannot fail, in seizing the occasion to speak, to transform directly and indirectly all systems of exchange based on masculine thrift. Her libido will produce far more radical effects of political and social change than one might like to think." (Cixous, *The Laugh of the Medusa*, in *New French Feminisms*, ed Elaine Marks & Isabelle de Courtivron, University of Massachusetts Press). Marguerite Duras argues that men and women live in different linguistic territories and write from radically different perspectives. Women must resist plagiarism of the masculine tradition, must resist taking off from a theoretical platform already in place, but must instead be translated from the unknown.

US critics, more grounded in praxis, argue for a modification of this radical otherness of woman's language: Showalter, for example, calls for a "feminist criticism that is genuinely woman-centred, independent, and intellectually coherent", but concludes that "women writing are not, then, inside and outside of the male tradition; they are inside two traditions simultaneously." From such a pragmatic position, one can argue that the novel, which as Bakhtin argues persuasively is the form that most offers possibilities for the multivocal, the polyphonic, the dialogical, the non-unitary and heteroglossic operations of language, would appear to be a woman's form that subverts the patriarchal institution of the monological, logocentric language of the male tradition.

Many feminists have appropriated the theme of difference, once used to oppress and subordinate women, and redeployed it to serve feminist purposes. There is something deeply seductive about a theory of language that dichotomises its properties through means of gender identification, and reverses the usual patriarchal social constructions that place male as superior and female as inferior. Woman's language, to follow through with this line of argument, is in its form closer to woman's lived experience, at the centre of which is the body. Ideas of otherness and the body are linked because the only visible differences between men and women is that of the body. This emphasis, however, may be dangerously essentialist, for "in today's context, with oppression not having ceased, to insist on Difference (without analyzing its social character) is to give back to the enemy a proven weapon." (Editors of *Questions Feministes,* 'Variations on some common themes', *Feminist Issues,* Summer 1980, p10) The illusory claim to Woman's language, the counter-theoreticians argue, is based on a current literary style that is just as academic and therefore as masculine as other literary languages. To claim that this language is closer to the body also implies an expression of the body that is not mediated by the social structure, thus denying the power of social mediations which give to feminist criticism its political edge. Radical feminists see it as their mission to attack the social roots of difference, including *ecriture feminine,* and define women as a class, sociologically defined in (from, within, by) a material and historical relation of oppression, but whose oppression is itself ideologically related by the dominant group to a so-called biological determination of the oppressed class (*ibid.,* p17).

Intersections

This radical definition of woman, resisting old or new mythologies of difference and insisting on a material analysis, is just as valid if we replace gender with race, specifically those people of colour who are minorities in white-majority societies, as African Americans in the US; or who are racial minorities in oppressive majority rule by other people of colour, as in Malaysia; or even a majority colonised by a minority race, as in South Africa. Minority or colonised race is a class, sociologically defined in a material and historical relation of oppression, whose oppression is itself ideologically related by a dominant group in a so-called biological determination of the oppressed class, and of that class alone.

As a Chinese Malaysian ethnic minority woman now resident in the United States, I cannot theorise the relation of language to gender without simultaneously incorporating the categories of class, race and nation. Reading Cixous, Irigaray, Showalter, Judith Newton, and, yes, even Alice Walker, bell hooks, and Barbara Smith, any number of European and American feminist writers on gender and language, I note how post-colonial, exilic, and third-world women of colour and their specific positions are continuously omitted[2]. Despite their theoretical interests in rethinking the category of woman outside the institutions of patriarchy, most feminist critics operate within many of these patriarchal structures without interrogation and with ease and privilege. National identities and borders, formed by a history of male wars, agents and interests, confer on these women safe within their borders, securities, powers and material advantages seldom disavowed.

Similarly, in their focus on language as the field of the female subject and as directly related to the speaking body of the woman, continental feminists frequently forget that the female body in other places is still the possession of patriarchal economic powers, is still a slave without voice and without subject identity. Rather than a site of pleasure, of autonomous defiance and disruption of patriarchal institutions, the female body in most societies is still the locus of alienation, of male rape and pleasure and female pain, disease, and unwanted child-bearing. Many European and American feminists do not ask how the pleasures of their language, their utopian feminist projects, are perhaps related to the material dystopias, the awful and increasing silence from the majority of women, but chiefly women of colour, in the world.

While it is important to ask whose language is it that is associated with colonial depredation or neo-colonial rapacity, while it is also important to ask who is doing the speaking, we should also ask what is being said. If it is important that women are finally speaking, writing and publishing, claiming their subject positions, overthrowing the mastery of the logocentric that had suppressed their female identities, we must also ask what is it that women are speaking. If "patriarchal power rests on the social meanings given to biological sexual difference" (Chris Weedon, *Feminist Practice and Poststructuralist Theory*, Basil Blackwell, 1987, p 2), then does Western feminist power rest on the social meanings given to racial, national and class difference? Feminist theory seeks to explain how and why people oppress each other; it is "a theory of subjectivity, of conscious and unconscious thoughts and emotions, which can account for the relation between the individual and the social." (*ibid.*, p 3) Feminist

2. Gayatri Chakravorty Spivak, *In Other Worlds: Essays in Cultural Politics* (London, Methuen, 1987); *The Post-Colonial Critic*, ed Sarah Harasym (New York, Routledge, 1990); and *Third World Women and the Politics of Feminism*, ed Chandra Talpade Mohanty, Ann Russo and Lourdes Torres (Bloomington, Indiana University Press, 1991), among more rcent books, do address the position of the post-colonial, "Third World" woman.

48

theory, therefore, must enlarge to include categories of race, nation and class, to account for the construction or destruction of subjectivity. If this 'burden of woman's content' merely replicates the pleasures of Western bourgeois literature, without expanding and breaking down those global boundaries that keep poor, disaffiliated women of colour in disintegrating national economies in their places, then this women's language is both complicit with and corrupted by those very patriarchal institutions from which it seeks to separate itself.

To return to the beginning of the meditation, the position of the exilic woman of colour attempting to maintain her grip on the circulation of knowledge that girds any strategy of power in the academy today while defending the language choice by which she has made her entry into this academy and while sceptical of the relation between her gender and that language as theorised by some of the major producers of that knowledge she is consuming – that position demonstrating such a narrow specificity as to raise intrusive issues of representation – who is speaking, what language is she speaking in, what is she speaking of – that is a position that may be taken to deconstruct or reconstruct other women's positions. If we believe that such a position would be more representative were it located in a native and national discourse, then we must acknowledge our privileging of political and patriarchal systems of nationalism and mythologising of essentialist origins. If we hold that the subject position would have more force of representation were it situated in a class node, for example a Third World service or working class, then we acknowledge that class supersedes, indeed forms the material base for subjectivity, and the gendered position is disqualified. Speaking as a woman in the interstice of class (in but not of an academic élite), race (a minority in a majority culture), and nation (of Chinese ancestry in a Malay-dominant nation-state; and an exile-immigrant in a dominant native-born Caucasian society), I note that certain versions of the native and of the relations between language, the native, and woman, hold more social and institutional sway than others. If I am painfully aware of the non-representational conclusion to be drawn from the specificity of my location, this awareness is also an articulate consciousness of how specificity resists the pressure of institutional explanations, and so resists the replacement of the individual woman with her universalised and canonised figure as third-world victim, which is the way that the woman of colour is put into Western discourse. Speaking as I do from the precarious position of discourse contradictions and resistances, I am subordinate both within and outside dominant cultures and ideologies. My position as exilic/immigrant third world woman is inherently marginal, marginalised ironically by my use of an international language, and marginalised in the discourse of feminism in the United States, where I make my second home, by my other identities in the categories of race, class, and nation.   *Shirley Geok-lin Lim*

Editor's note: for a full list of references in this article, send SAE/IRC to *Chapman*.

Shuntaro Tanikawa

On Sending People Poems

You can't give poems to anyone.
They cannot be owned
like neckties.
From the moment they're written they belong
neither to me nor you but to everyone.
Whatever your beautiful dedication,
however private the memories you reveal,
poems cannot be hidden from the public eye.
Since they are not even the poet's possessions
they can belong to anyone,
like the world
which belongs to no one and everyone.
Poems weave like the breeze between people.
They light up in a lightning flash the face of truth.
Though the poet tries to hide his lover's name
in an acrostic, his aspiration
transcends the poem's local meaning
and he cannot imprison his poem even in his own volume.
Sending people poems is like
sending people air.
If air, I'd wish it were the silent air
that spills from lover's lips.
For we long for souls' communion
in which words are not yet words
and yet no longer words,
words piling up word upon word upon word.

Tempter-Tree

Trees don't care what people think;
they just lift their leaves skyward.
They bloom, scatter their seeds
and adding a growth-ring every year
outlive people by far,
and, having at long last turned bone-white,
wither and die ‑ they're such incredible chaps
that you should never let your guard down.
Their roots seize our souls
and never let go.
Their young leaves shatter sunlight
and entrance lovers.
Their trunks wear blank faces,

indifferent to any tyrant's history.
And their shadows make pilgrims
in any age dream of paradise.
Trees with their greenness tease our eyes
into the world beyond,
and, with their great branches spread out,
embrace our noisy future.
Their leaves rustle rumours in our ears,
the eternal whispering of lovers.

We must stand in awe of trees,
because they are irresistible tempters.
Because they are far nearer to God than we are,
we should pray to them.

Easy Listening

In a stone building built 300 years ago
in a hall whose ceiling was painted with dancing angels,
the music was played and recorded (perhaps for eternity).

But people will perish in time.
And even if I stop lamenting the fact,
my soul may not wander in Hades when I'm dead,
because devils, too, perish with us anyway.

The Duchess's slim ankles that glided so gracefully
to a slow saraband are now white bones...
Let's stop this endless speculation.

Only those longings lurking in an unforgettable melody
deserve to be called 'reality'.
From somewhere, neither hell nor paradise, a voice calls me
with a bright, almost dying tremolo.

Breakfast Duet

Stared at by the fried egg, she blushed.
He felt awkward because the ham was listening.
They were doing nothing unusual
but it seemed like a dreadful secret.

Spiders in the trees are eating butterflies;
the water in the distant valley is eating the river-banks;
one idea in a man's mind is eating another.
Eating resembles loving.

Last night, whispering, "I want to devour you,"
she made love to him by way of repaying her egg
to this dazzling world.

Hunger and Books

There are places filled with people
by the tens of thousands, and not a single book;
and places filled with as many books,
and only one person.
John said there ought to be edible books
so people could eat them after they had finished them,
but then, they would eat them before reading if they were starving.
I wish I were on the edge of a cliff.
I'd have a single volume
and I'd read it aloud.
I mean, what we have kept writing and call books
I'd read out to the sea and sky.

Spring

A soft sea breeze blows in from the south
and distant mountains hide behind a curtain.
Though I'm not a man of the soil
but only handle the shape of characters,
if I lay down my not-so-busy pen and close my eyes
I can envision spring.

The time when men and women have used arms and legs,
and have joined their wisdom and forces
to produce their own food and clothing is now passing.
We now play with money, in a cold sweat,
constantly seeking pleasure instead of joy,
cold isolation instead of anger.

You vanished into Hades long ago.
I'd really like to talk with you,
but what would we talk about?
Here I lie late abed this morning,
reading old poems filled with bird songs,
and those voices are critical of me.

Translated by William I Elliott & Kazuo Kawamura

aonghas macneacail

walkman ok?

mise

dé cho deàrrsach
's a bhiodh do shaoghal
nan robh do chluasan dùinte
do chàil ach ceòl

nach fàsadh e
mar shàbh air cloich
mar thàirngrean fuaime
brag nan tiompan
gaoir nam feadan
an àite briathran
gu sìorruidh sìorruidh

guth eile

ach éisd, ged tha, 's
bheir triobhualadh teud thu
suas gu na speuran
is glaodh nam fìdeag
mar fuarain bùirn
agus piàno piàno
anns gach cànan
a togail 's a teàrnadh
tuireannadh's a taomadh
sgann ghealbhoinn
am broilleach gréine

agus éisd, ged tha, an
d'rinn uiseag nan cluaintean
càil riamh ach seinn
agus éisd, ged tha, ri
ceòl do chuislean
fhad's is bualadh beò dhut
bodhràn do chridhe

coisich tromh choille
do smuaintean fhéin
leig an oiteag
ameasg an duillich,
is cluinn
air a mhol mhór
an cuan a diogladh nan clach

walkman ok?

me

*how radiant
would your world be
if your ears were closed to
all but music*

*wouldn't it get
like a saw on stone
like rivets of sound
the snaredrum's rattle
the trumpet's bleat
instead of words
for ever ever*

another voice

*but listen though
the strings' vibration
will lift you skyward
and the whistle's call
like freshest springs
and piano piano
in any language
raising, descending
incandescent, spilling
a flock of sparrows on
the sun's bright breast*

*and listen though, did
the lark of the meadows
ever stop singing
and listen though, to
the music of your veins
while you hear the pulse
of your heart's bodhràn*

*walk through the forest
of your thoughts and
let the breeze go
through the leaves
and hear
on the shingle beach
the ocean tickling the stones*

mise
aon fhacal deireannach, ged tha
ged tha, cha b'ann
stopte na do chluais
guth eile
nach dèan thu fead

me
one last word, though
not stuffed
in your ears, though
another voice
why don't you whistle

smachd

dé chluinneas mi
dé chluinneas mi
chan è mo ghuth fhìn
no guth mo nàbaidh
ach guth coimheach eòlach
a chosg airgiod
's e 'g ràdha riùm
cha dèan thu riaghladh
ged nach can e guth
's tha fhios aig a ghuth
direach dé tha e dèanamh
ged nach aidich e
dha fhéin e...
cha leig e leas

control

what do i hear
what do i hear
not my own voice
nor my neighbour's voice
but a strange familiar voice
that's been paid for
which says to me
you can't rule
though it says nothing
and the voice knows
exactly what it is doing
though not admitting
to itself...
it doesn't need to

dòchas
25mh dhen fhaoilleach 1993

an dearbh latha
fhuair alba saorsa
dh'éirich gleadhair
ameasg nam bàrd
air có b'fheàrr, air
feadh an t-saoghail

cluinn na briathran seo:
ma tha 'n crùn ri fhaotainn
b'fhiach strì air a shon
ged a dh'fhàgadh an strì
taobh eile na dìg e

an dearbh latha
fhuair alba saorsa
dh'éirich gleadhair
mus do bhuail an uair –

rabhadh bàird.

cauld kail het again

hope
25th january 1993

the very day
scotland won freedom
an uproar arose
among the poets
anent who was best, in
all the world

hear these words:
if there's a crown to be gained
it's worth fighting for
though the fight should leave
it beyond the dyke

the very day
scotland won freedom
an uproar arose
before the clock had struck –

a poet's warning.

cauld kail het again

ri linn nan crócus

ri linn nan crócus a bhi
togail sleaghan sìtheil nan dath
is na calmain fhathast
a sireadh an t-seann arain
agus daonnan na h-aodainn cràiteach
balbh, ann an uinneagan sanntach nan telefis
gun diù dha na sùilean gan coimhead
tromh na h-uinneagan craosach ud
is na sùilean air am bleith mìn
le eòlas nan dealbh brònach
agus bathair nam margaidh-calpa
agus clàr-reice nan clàr
agus tomadachd latha nam prionnsa
agus buill-coise air cuairt na h-iarmailt,
tha na calmain cho loma-làn 's nach gluais iad
le coimhneas nan cailleach
agus seall gach crócus air fuasgladh
cuach dòchais,
fan gus an lìonar iad – an è
stòp fiona, stòp fala

in the season when crocuses

in the season when crocuses
raise peaceful spears of colour
and the doves still
peck at old bread
and always the anguished faces
dumb, in the ravenous windows of televisions
indifferent to the eyes watching them
through those voracious windows
and the eyes are ground smooth
being so used to the pitiful scenes
and the stock-market reports
and the hit-parades
and the burdensome days of princes
and footballs in orbit,
the doves are so glutted they cannot move
with the kindness of old women
and see the crocus opening
a cup of hope,
but wait till it fills – is it
wine, is it blood

aonghas macneacail

Translations by John Manson

Pablo Neruda

Pardon if by my eyes...

Pardon if by my eyes I come to
no more light than the spume of the sea,
pardon because my space
extends without protection
and does not end:
monotonous is my song,
my word is a dark bird,
fauna of stone and of sea, the disconsolation
of a winter planet, incorruptible.
Pardon this succession of water,
rock, spume, delirium
of the tide: so is my solitude:
sudden showers of salt against the walls
of my own self, in such a way
that I am a part
of winter,
of the very deeps which swell again
from bell to bell in so many waves
and of a silence like a tress,
silence of seaweed, submarine song.

From *El Mar y Las Campanas*, 1973

I want to know...

I want to know if you're coming with me
not to walk and talk, I want
to know if in the end we'll understand
the lack of communication: at last
to go with someone to see the clear air,
the striped light on the everyday sea
or a landmark
and to have nothing to interchange
at last, not to bring in commodities
as the colonists used to do
exchanging trinkets for silence.
I pay here for your silence.
Agreed: I give you mine
on one condition: not to understand each other.

From *El Mar y Las Campanas*, 1973

Umberto Saba

Broken Gless

Aathing gangs aganist ye, cours wether,
licht lek the white o an eigg,
the auld hous rattled bi a shouer o hail
and close til ye for aa ye gaed throu,
houps mistrysted,
for some guid things ony wey.
Ye think that til pull throu
is til gang aganist aa the odds.
        And in the tinglan
o the gless in the winda is the doom.

Frae *Ultime Cose*, 1935–43

Francisco Vallverdu

Oath

I swear not to insult my very small country
which like a hungry child has not grown,
I swear not to curse this cramped language
understood by four cats and the poet.
I promise not to dream of other larger countries,
not to reject the bitter gall of Catalonia.
I take you for a witness, you who read Catalan,
from now on, that's the end of the spleen.
I have simply changed the scale of values
because the wish to serve is stronger than the pain,
because I have only one country as well,
and if I want to flee, I only have the moon.

via *Les Lettres Françaises*, 22–28 February 1962

Jon Úr Vör

Blin Horse

Thae wha had een
At Hiroshima
Saw a blin horse,
Hinderend reiddened bi the fire,
Tail and mane burnt aff

Rin throu
The ruinage o the toun
And Daith hersel
Didna daur
Get on his back

Original language Icelandic, translated into French by Régis Boyer
(*Europe* 647, March 1983) – *John Manson*

The Scottish Language Project

Robbie Robertson

Astonishingly enough, the language curriculum found around Scotland is an alien place for our native languages. Even optimists would be forced to say that the Scots language has been *almost* invisible in Scottish schools. The situation of Scots literature is only a little different, although Anglo-Scottish literature is happily more thriving. The teaching of Gaelic literature in translation and the provision of an awareness of Gaelic itself (certainly outside the Highlands, Islands and wee bits of Strathclyde) is so far below the horizon there is scarce a glimmer in the night.

Addressing and redressing such deficits have been preoccupations over decades for writers, teachers, broadcasters, parents and cultural theorists. Central agencies such as the Scottish Office Education Department, the Scottish Examination Board, colleges of education, universities, the education authorities themselves, as well as the group I work for, the Scottish Consultative Council on the Curriculum, can claim, with hands on their hearts, that the advice, guidance and support they have offered, certainly over the last twenty-five years or so, consistently promotes and sustains the teaching of Scottish language and literature in schools. Other, more immediately interested bodies such as the Association for Scottish Literary Studies, the Saltire Society, and the Scots Language Society have offered support too, and there are many teachers in primary and secondary schools who teach in these areas with a consistent record of achievement. Yet, despite these positive signs, at a *national* level success in making Scots and Gaelic an everyday feature of schoolwork has been scant, progress at best slow, sometimes non-existent.

Against that background comes the new Scottish Language Project. Because nothing comes from nowhere, it builds on and complements the labours over the years of those other people and organisations already mentioned. The Project brings the Scottish Consultative Council on the Curriculum (CCC) into partnership with all of Scotland's education authorities. The common effort will be to promote the use of Scots, and Gaelic with translations, in all primary and secondary schools.

The background

Any effort such as the Scottish Language Project has to be developed with some awareness of both the curricular and cultural situation it is set in. Only in this way can what is needed and what is feasible be properly gauged. The Project is, of course, engaged in a struggle against history, and difficult questions have to be asked. *Can* the curriculum help to reverse the present situation? Should it try? If yes, *what* should be done – and how?

Certainly, the lack of attention to Scots and Gaelic in a high proportion of Scottish schools is a significant absence, and should be read as arising from intention rather than neglect or accident. These intentions need not have been verbalised or fully understood; the decisions accompanying them might not even have been consciously taken – they might have emerged from what seemed to be the right way to go at certain times. The question *Teach Scots and Gaelic in schools?* might not have been asked because "clearly" these were languages of little merit, and, had it been asked, the response would inevitably have been a disparaging snigger.

Who made, or did not make, such decisions will usually be of lesser significance than the conditions which produced them. Once taken, each decision inevitably influenced every other decision, and the greater the number of decisions to move (or not to move) in a particular direction, the greater the likelihood, sometimes the certainty, of similar decisions being made in the future. These decisions emerged from sets of historical contingencies of advantage to one broad alignment of cultural interests. In considering what these contingencies might be there is a cast of hundreds. Economic considerations? Shame? Gradualist cultural diffusion? A sense of insignificance, maybe inferiority, in the shadow of a brilliant dialect fast becoming a common tongue for the planet and which has been pervading Scots from at least the 17th century onwards? The mass media? The cultural clout of the USA? Technology generally?

The failure of Scots and Gaelic to develop new words to maintain their connection with a rapidly transforming culture breeding concepts and innovations both material and immaterial pell-mell? Also, losing Scots, forgetting Gaelic, would bring few social or economic disadvantages for writers, readers, manufacturers – anybody in fact focused on a world outside Scotland. Why speak a minority language when an enormous English-speaking world is waiting?

The significance of education and educators in such smothering processes is certainly no different from that of other transmitters and promoters of views such as the churches, professions, the bourgeoisie, the arts, the political process, and the mass media. An intent shared by such institutions is especially powerful because they are cohesive controllers not only of debate but of what is *allowed* to be debated. They run the agenda, and establishing points of view contrary to their interests is always difficult. At certain times in history it was impossible. Despite a more pluralist culture, the same is only slightly less true now.

Moments when decisions about Scots and Gaelic were taken, or not taken, would help to fix that common view. Dictionaries to stabilise or authenticate the language? A consistent, coherent literary language used by whom and with what standing? Translations of the Bible, in what language, when, where, how often, and used by whom? The language of legal statutes? The currency of "polite" discourse that would give Scots (and Gaelic) authority? When they first appeared, became less prevalent, disappeared, or if they have not appeared at all, are always significant indicators of cultural transformations.

To make the loss invisible, unproblematic, and any argument about it wearisome, such an obliteration of history and language (in this context the two are almost mirrors of each other) would be naturalised, made acceptable, invisible. This might be done through the popular arts, the nature of employment, fashion, role-models, education, and social interchanges of other kinds including the micro-commerce of everyday lives, to mention only a few.

In television and the press, for example, Scots is now universally acceptable only in comedy and comic strips. This acceptability extends to England. Very rarely is Scots given the high ground of news, features, and cultural debate. Then it is often objectified, turned into Other, constituted as a problem, a difficulty or an irritation obstructing the smooth flow of culture. Radio is only marginally different. Its narrow casting permits sensitive issues about culture and language to be corralled into frequencies listened to by smaller (and usually older) audiences. Such a location presents no significant threat to the authority and integrity of the dominant linguistic culture, and to the values inscribed within it.

In such communication structures the role of discourses – including language – in the formation of national identities is of central importance. For example, in visual cultures such as ours imagery is an important element in constructing "the real". Through these constructions varieties of issues are manufactured to create false or simplified realities – the always-kilted Highlander, the Scottish soldier (ditto), the wee hoose in the glen, the kailyard world of bothies, brose and bulls. Against the imagery of the modernist world Scots is seen as an unwelcome reminder of antique things best extinguished by forgetting, sentimentality or, worst of all, charm. Such meanings are made to mask rather than reveal, to mystify rather than illuminate, to stop time dead in an eternal Brigadoon.

In those discourses which are privileged and have prestige – standard English is one – empowerment is the aim. Other oppositional readings such as those created by the experiences of real people, are in the nowhere jungle, off the broad highways of mainstream culture, trivialised, functionless, disabled. This is true even of Scots itself, with the urban variant often relegated to an inferior position as if rural Scots were the only "authentic" tongue. Such divisions are part of that disempowering strategy to which most of us, always unconsciously, often subscribe.

The cases of Scots and Gaelic are only marginally different. Because Gaelic is a language on a different branch of the language tree it is able to assert its individuality – and pedigree – with more self-assurance. Arresting its decline, however, poses specific problems that cannot be solved by educational methods alone, although these are vital. Despite having cash spent on it, in Gaelic-medium education, in the mass media, in support for its arts, the situation is far from healthy and success not yet guaranteed. And the ill feeling that this largesse engenders among some Scots speakers can only be represented as one starving beggar struggling with another in a war for crumbs – yet another way, of course, to de-energise the debate and for certain interests to achieve their intentions.

A solution?

In mid-February 1993 all the Scottish education authorities agreed to take part in the Scottish Language Project in partnership with the CCC. What they agreed to can be described quite quickly: an *anthology* containing prose, poetry, drama, word games in both Gaelic in translation and Scots, together with visual texts such as comic strips, cartoons and pictures, and a *kist* of materials linked to the anthology. Both are intended for classrooms in upper primary and lower secondary schools.

The authorities will supply the texts for the anthology drawn from the dialects and resources in their part of Scotland, and write virtually all the classroom materials. The CCC will be responsible for co-ordination, design, manufacture and distribution. Publication of the anthology and the kist, in December 1994, will provide a focus for authorities to run a substantial in-service training programme to promote the teaching of Scots and Gaelic, literature and language. Developing national materials for this training programme is also on the Project's agenda.

Management is in the hands of a small group drawn from a spectrum of interests – primary and secondary schools, college of education, university, local authority, Saltire Society, and CCC; the interests of both Scots and Gaelic are represented.

All the Project's materials will be professionally designed and visually stimulating, making extensive use of colour and modern layout. There will be an emphasis on the contemporary although the past will not be forgotten. Any word or phrase likely to be of difficulty will be glossed alongside its appearance in the text – *that* is essential for young readers. The binding and packaging will be colourful and robust.

Each text in the anthology will have teaching materials related to it. These materials will be packed inside the kist and, like the anthology's texts themselves, will address a range of different needs and competences in language and provide sufficient work for a number of years. The kist will also contain audio tape readings of all the print texts in the anthology made by native speakers of Gaelic and each dialect of Scots. There will be a videotape showing the different locales in which Gaelic and the dialects of Scots occur. There will be a poster for the wall showing the histories of Scots and Gaelic, and a computer program to let schools author their own teaching materials to the same design as those in the kist.

The kist is growing. Things added mean, however, extra costs – a difficulty at a time of shrinking resources – but everything is agreed with each education authority. Now, for example, it may include a feature film with teaching notes and activities. Link-ups with the BBC are being explored, and other inclusions on the horizon.

One central aim of the Project is to develop a clearer perception of what Scots and Gaelic are, why they should be valued and what they can offer us *now*. It must work in partnership with, rather than attack, standard English in schools. A common dialect across the British Isles, and indeed the world, clearly has advantages and to argue against it would be preposterous. Giving a command of how to read and communicate in the standard dialect, and an appreciation of those texts which use it, must be a central activity of any educational process worthy of the name. The development of such skills must begin from the first day of school because, despite currently fashionable mythologies, they have *never* been caught readily no matter the time, the methods and the effort put into developing them.

Giving attention to Scots, Gaelic *and* English has many advantages. For example, one difficulty of promoting more imaginative forms of textual study and language awareness is that a teaching system which uses only one language cannot readily make comparisons. Without a range of languages we cannot effectively teach what language is, and what its histories are. We cannot teach about the social situations, and societies, which produce different or related languages, the ways languages merge, borrow from each other; we cannot give an understanding of those occasions when different forms of language are appropriate or inappropriate; we will find it difficult to teach the nature of dialects, where slang fits in, and how they relate to the standard dialect; and, finally, we cannot teach *why* a command of language is important.

In these endeavours Scotland has a major advantage in having three languages within its boundaries, English, Scots (a cousin) and Gaelic (effectively unrelated). This diversity is a great richness and that we have not leapt to exploit it is an indication of the power of those obfuscating forces we have inherited. Soon, a modern European language will also be a commonplace in the curriculum of primary schools. Community ethnic languages like Cantonese or Urdu are increasingly being added to the curricular pot. From monoglot we are heading towards, and in some cases have arrived at, polyglot schools. The exciting perceptions of language and learning that such situations permit can only be of value for the individual, the curriculum and society as a whole.

Accommodating our native languages within this new framework is becoming increasingly natural; the teaching of Scots and Gaelic now has powerful allies. Throughout this century evidence has been accumulating from socio- and psycholinguistics of the importance of language in the formation of personal as well as social identities. Forcing one dialect on top of another, privileging one at the expense of another, does not create a unified concept of language, or, more importantly, of the self. Such a crude approach can set up barriers – doubt, uncertainty, diffidence and apprehension arising from earlier scholastic "failures" – between the homes of a community and their schools that travel across generations. This approach also impedes learning by producing distorted perceptions of what is valued and why. More sinister, it can also create additional learning difficulties for children whose acquisition of language is proving difficult, by making their natural linguistic abilities seem worthless.

The Project suggests a more coherent approach. Although its materials are aimed at upper primary and lower secondary classes there is some likelihood that using them will have other forms of effect both earlier and later in the school. The national guidelines on English Language at ages 5 to 14 (published by the Scottish Office) stress the importance of welcoming and building on the language the youngest children bring to school, and the guidelines, in common with others on later stages (also published by the Scottish Office), promote the value of Scots and Gaelic in the curriculum.

The Project will support such views. The years of 10 to 14 are the keystone of the bridge, and providing an awareness of the wealth of Scots and Gaelic for these middle years is also likely to influence and lead to a revaluation of their place in the curriculum for language and literature at Standard and Higher Grades, and beyond.

The questions

Things *are* changing but the central question, perhaps the only question, posed by the analysis remains: what can education do against the obliterations and omissions of the past which now have been naturalised and made acceptable? The answer is brutal and short: virtually nothing. There is no quick way to unwind the spool of history (there may not be a slow way either). Such matters are certainly beyond the scope of the educational process and let us be happy that this is so, for, were it otherwise, would it provide anything other than tyranny?

What education can attempt is to ensure that children are given such intellectual and personal tools as logical and creative thinking, a sense of values and discrimination, a feeling for community and the needs of others, that will eventually allow them to determine what the options are, or should be, and then, out of an awareness of the issues and the likely nature of the consequences, make their decisions.

Language teaching can assist such processes. It can also ensure that it does not impede them through the endorsement of past mistakes. So far as Scots and Gaelic are concerned the Project can reveal their quality, develop an understanding of their contributions to culture, provide them with the dignity of a place in the curriculum and its activities, and so accord them status. The Project may also begin the task of demystifying and explaining those processes which created the situation we now find ourselves in. Enhancement of consciousness is a heavy phrase but that is a major part of what education has to be about.

But achieving any significant arrestment in the decline of Scots and Gaelic will require that the whole of education acts in concert with the loudest voices in our society – the great writers and artists, the mass media, those role models followed by the young, the traffic of daily discourse, among others.

Such ambitions are, however, far beyond the Project which will add only a few sentences, at best a paragraph, to the broad narrative of culture. But let's say it again: things *are* changing. Although the analysis outlined at the beginning is bleak there are signs that the issues it identifies are being addressed. There is a growing sense of Scottish identity, of what has been lost, a feeling that things need not be as they are, that the past is not unredeemable – and, significantly, this is a feeling growing among the young. Finally, and happily, this mood seems to transcend party politics whose competing interests often result only in fragmentation and further distraction. *Robbie Robertson*

Gerry Cambridge

An Old Crofter Speaks

Oa, cum an in an doan't stand at thee doar!
I doan't get meny cum ti see me noo.
Here, sit thee doon. Ah, that must be where
Wun o me cats browt in a rabbit, luk,
Last night. I try ti stap them doin it,
But that's chust hoo they're made. Yaas, yaas.
That is chust hoo they're made. As you kin see,
I'm nat much o a hoosekeeper. Until
Me mither died, in nineteen eighty-two,
She wid tek care o that fer me, but noo
Thee hoal thing is chust leaft ti do mesel.
As weel as which this dwellin's noo so oald
It's finisht aboot wi dampness, an
Winniver I hev dun wi beasts ootside, it's aall
I manidge ti mek me food, an chust sit here.
I s'poase I shood hee merreed. Ah, but there
Wus nat a single wooman here wid tek me.
Why shood that be, man? Nat a single wun.
It may be it wus me oan falt, afore
I understood chust hoo. It aall began
When I wus in me teens. They'd hoald
A dance doon in thee haall each Setterday.
(There wus much moar foak livin here than noo.)
Me faather wus thee fiddler, an becaas
I wus ashayemd ti dance a front o him,
I nivver danced at aall, I nivver gat
Over me fear o dancin, an sumtimes
I think it aall stems bek ti that. Thee weemun,
Why, they were aff wi aall thee ither men
Who'd dance, y'see, so I wus leaft mesel.
Oa, Jean Breckness affert wunce ti tek me,
Two hooses farther Narth, but that wus bek
In nineteen sixty-sevan, when her foaks
Hed died. Bluddy hell, that wus no yoose ti me;
Why, she coodna hev carreed chuldren,
She wus chust too oald. Whut yoose wus that ti me?
Oa aye, I went ti her aall right, until
She toald me she'd two ither men, who came
Visitin on her reggular, an did I meet wun
Anytime? Why, bluddy hell, I thowt
Why wid I waant ti meet wun foar, ti ask
Er ti be toald if she went well thee night?

So I stapped goin then, y'see, becaas
Thee ither two were merreed, an I thowt
If sumthin heppened her, I might end up
Hevvin ti raise a yung un nat me oan.
It wid be moar respectabul if she
Cood point ti me, y'see, a batcheller.
But anyway, we didna waant each ither.
There's nivver been a wooman here I'd waant
That aalso waanted me. Oa, o coorse it wid
Hee made me happy, man. O coorse it wid.
Ah, but that's dun noo. Oa, I cood hee leaft
When duzzens o yung weemun leaft, when thee
Last waar wus an, an nat cum bek, but then
Me foaks hed no wun here ti wurk thee craaft,
An waanted me ti stay. An so I stayed
Y'see, but aall thee weemun leaft, an moast
Nivver came bek at aall. Bluddy hell, an why
Shood they cum bek, ti this hoal o a place,
This hoal o a smaall island? Sumtimes I think
That even hed they dun so, it wid nat
Hev changed things in thee least. I s'poase I mean
I've allus been quite shy, an then thee moar
I liked a wooman, why, thee shyer I
Becayem. Hoo do you mek oot that wun?
Yoor thee intellekchul, man, nat me.
Is that nat chust reedeecullus? You wid hee thowt
Thee apposite shood be thee case, an yit
It nivver wus wi me, an aall becaas
O bluddy shyness. (This is thee drink
Taalkin thee night, I s'poase; oa, sumtimes,
I wish I cood hee been drunk aall thee time,
Wi'oot thee bad eefects o coorse, becaas
Thee drink taalks moar than I cood manidge
Ivver.)
Er we nat hevvin chust a fine
Time o it thegither? Ah, but it must end,
It must cum ti an end. Oa, rownd aboot
Thee sixties there, when I cood wurk oot hoo
Thee hoal thing hed ti end, it gat so bad,
Me depresshan gat so bad, I chust hed
Ti see thee dactor. I felt I cood haardly
Do anythin at aall, me mind wus chust,
Oa, chust aboot entiyerly seized up. Yaas.
So I hev hed whut you wid caall a moast
Unsuccessfool life. Oa, bluddy hell,
I canna see hoo you mek that oot!
Lats an lats o foaks seem heppier than me.

Why, when aall they visiturs cum here an say
'This is a luvlee island', aall I kin say's
'It hasna been sae bewtifool ti me.'

That's why I hev ti drink so much, y'see.
Chust drink an lie here blatto, yaas, chust lie
Here bluddy blatto, on me oan. Cood I
Hev fownd a wooman, I'd nat hev needed that.
Why, even if wun o they yung wuns, that cums
Visitin this smaall island, affert me
Her bady, likelee it's too late. Yaas, yaas.
I've lawest me tinkul, I'm chust dun.
No like you, you've gat a lat leaft in you yit.
But lissun ti me noo, yoor time is lumutud.
Lum-u-tud. Go ti it man, while yoove thee chaance!
You waant ti end up sum oald man like me,
Sum oald drunk man like me? I'll soon be gan,
I'll soon be in me bluddy bax, you'll hev
Ti taalk wi me up at thee kirkyaard, there.
Hoo deep hev they ti dig? Oa, chust deep enuff
Ti mek shoor that you'll nat climb oot again.
That needna be too deep, o coorse, at aall.
Yaas, yaas, I've dug sum mesel; they ask
Thee friends ti dig thee grave, y'see. Hoo deep?
Oa, wi thee last wun there, I think I mind
After thee furst foot it gat exsepshanally saaft,
So we were doon ti thee roape-ends afore
Anywun realised it; yooshally it's nat
So deep, fer if there bees a lat o rocks
An stoanes, sumwun or ither yooshally
Suggests we mek it do. But it may be
We aalso thowt that when his sister dies
She cood be put in o thee tap o him,
Ti save moar wurk. That's mebbe whut we thowt,
Fer she'll nat live forivver. Sum jaab that,
Diggin throo oald bits o boanes an teeth –
Fer it's teeth last thee langest. Yaas, yaas.

Oa, bluddy hell, you doan't believe aall that!
Manshuns in thee sky! If you think so,
Chump in thee sea tomarrow! Oa, chust go
An chump inti thee sea! But when I go
Up ti thee hoose an Mundy, you'll be there.
An tell me why is that? Becaas you know
That no such place exists. It exists here?
You like ti look at clowds? Oa aye.
Cut oot aall that reeleejan stuff wi me!
Hev I nat toald you that afoar? Aall that

Is chust preetenshasness, reeleejan's chust
A pack o bluddy lies! Ah, but you doan't
Mean it as thee ithers do, o coorse.

Lissun, man, chust lissun ti me noo.
I mind when me faather an me unkul wus alive.
Me unkul wus a teacher, whut you'd caall
A skallar; when he were yung he nivver hed
His face oot o a book; he's deid, o coorse.
Me faather went ti see him in thee haspeetal.
His belly wus aall swoallen up, an he
Lifted bek thee cuvvers so's ti show
Me faather hoo it wus; me faather wus disgustet.
Me faather hed an intrest in astronomy.
He liked ti go oot an a night, an luk
Away up at thee staars. But anyhoo,
Him an me unkul, they wid sit sum nights
Away inti thee smaall oors in that hoose
Doon at thee shoar, discussin aall them things.
It's empty noo; full o rats an slaters. Anyhoo,
When I wus smaall I'd lissun. Bluddy hell,
Sumtimes they'd try ti taalk away thee night!
Thee thing aboot it wus, it leaft them no
Wiser than afoar. So I thowt I'd
Chust save mesel thee trubble, an ferget
Aboot they soarts o things, so that's thee road
I tuk an hev stuck ti.
                    Will you nat stay
An tek anither pint wi me at least?
Ah, you hev ti go; it'll be dark be noo.
You hev til waalk a few miles yit, ti bed.
Me oan bed is chust here. Thanks anyhoo,
Fer visitin.
                    Will you mind o these nights?
Will you mind o these nights when I'm nat here?
We might nat hee been sittin like this, were
Me faather nat thee fiddler. Ah, but I
Wus frightened they wid laff at me, y'see.
I'll allus wish I'd bluddy danced when yung.

Tree Destiny

Cables like fence-wires strung on sky
And hanging near-taut from arms of giants
Suddenly gleaming in this green place
If crying worked, might make you cry.

They caused a dozen unwept deaths,
The crackling and irreversible fall
(One for every month of the year)
Of trees whose fault was growing tall.

If it's the fault to reach such size
That it would seem to be, for scrub,
Diminutive enough, was spared,
As if such smallness was most wise.

I'd never have thought that such was so!
But then I watched near-helpless men
Crowd-charged, cut the beeches down
That cannot help the height to which they grow.

And now, here, an innocent might miss
What appears to me disease.
An innocent might not guess
That twelve stiff pylons were once trees.

Millions Wouldn't

I sense you're sad when I say, 'let's be friends,
Not more'; as I am sad, when you agree;
Yet both relieved also, imagining
Now we needn't broach our faults, nor ends
Plot. A prospect changed in seconds! And we
Need not test now the merest brush of lips,
The long love-looks, smiles, touching of fingertips,
And the whole riveting night-enlarging thing.
Just friends. Ah absolutely. This is quite
Beyond a question now. So buried deep
At last, those old sweet-devious plotters, and
Near-shut what we can barely understand,
That sea-disclosing door ajar of 'might'.
But ah, heaven help us if we peep.

From a Hilltop

I paint the kitchen doors fresh cherry red
This autumn day, leaving the mind's concerns:
Unconstrained, the mind emptily burns,
So today I love this, sweetly-limited,
Painting with a wet-bright brush, empty my head,
As sunlight enters; and Earth hugely turns
This room, far cities, forests, their golden ferns,
That mock with a sheer reality all that's said.

And when I step outside the amazing light
Ignites the miles of gold-frail and earth-strong
Woods to brilliance on the clouds' black-bright;
And the heart dances to reality's song,
As all the miles eastward charge the sight.
Listen if you dare, but never long!

The Shell House

When I was younger and the world wide, I sought
The fabulous bird that was over each next skyline;
Here, there, near, far, for twenty empty years
Ignored each simple linnet's nest to roam
Valley and hilltop on a timeless quest;
And came at last to a linnet's clutch,
Five eggs speckled in the lined cup,
And held one up to space; admitting the light,
Frail, the white shell glowed, vessel for cosmic gold;
And so I reached the first, last, place,
And distant-travelled rays their dazzling home.

Gerry Cambridge

Maurice Lindsay

Highland Waterfall

With shadow hands the clouds caressed two hills
divided by a gully. Rained-out spills,
oozing through sphagnum moss, the roots of ferns,
gathered their peaty coolness into burns
that pulsed and twisted to a running pace
momentum-high above a rocky face.

Beneath, I watched the weight of water falling
into itself, the roar to echo calling;
across the spray and spitter sunlight shone
fragments of rainbow broken over stone;
pieces of not belonging, flotsam-free,
with leaves and twigs frothed brownwards to the sea.

Toys Are Us

Pop, goes the toddler's cork on a short string;
crack, smokes the pistol's cap in schoolboy fun;
a feathered pellet flies with the rifle's *ping*;
death grape-shots from a double-barrelled gun
on wild, defenceless things. Toy soldiers bring
legends to bygone battles, lost or won.
Grimed actors in heroic poses sing
of battle's glories, enemies on the run.
We zap and splat each other in war games,
watch cops and robbers on the TV screen,
ambivalent as sometimes are their aims;
there's nowhere violent that we haven't been.
Fantasy playing real, for good or ill,
thus finds us well-prepared. We'll shoot to kill.

Read My Lips

The best soap-opera we'd ever seen
on television, though it wasn't suds
that flowed when rockets failed to meet the Scuds,
or pilots roared the darkness off our screen,
or bombs breached targets and the streets between,
or knocked-out tanks lay belching twisted flames
as generals, accustomed to war games,
explained with diagrams what it should mean.
A victory. The ruined country free.

But what it meant, it turned out, was quite other.
A tyrant left with genocide to smother
tribes who took up their challenged liberty
half-promised by a politician's word
the unsaid half of which declared absurd.

Old Sir William

He led the pitiless fields of industry with the flash of his name,
force-marching his abilities far beyond the common reach,
dominating sherry-tabled boardrooms, the TV game
of prophesying weekly where some unlikely probing breach
might salient recession, or strike with counter-flanking slump
and overrun the thin-held line of a too-relaxed prosperity.
He hadn't counted human figures when he came to dump
wastelands of campaigned unemployed, the casualties of severity.
Far from the distant-sounding fronts, the forces he commanded,
the chequebook lunches, applauded speechy dinners, he lies, spoon-fed
on minced-up munchings, the ruthless bric-a-brac of his dignity stranded
limply upon the rubber-sheeted stench of a wet bed,
matted with words, the worry-beads of forgotten half-conversations.
Old age, the sprucing nurse observed, *is no respecter of persons.*

Televising Christmas Eve

A crowd colours the stone-grey square around
an illuminated phallic Christmas tree;
everyone singing, as if they'd suddenly found
what harking herald angels ought to be:
a new beginning; a clean line drawn beneath
private mistakes, betrayals; what sharing a feast
can sometimes purify – like laying a wreath
on a monument to the publicly deceased.
Curlicued high on buildings, the pink feet
of pigeons balance, whitening niche and spar,
sheening their necks to jerk a flick-eyed view
over the noisome difference in the street:
creatures who don't know where or what they are,
peering at those below who think they do.

Impromptu X: Whippet for High Tea

Heh Jimmy, listen. Here's a bluidy guid yin.
Some fucker's left a copy o *The Times*
on the table. It sez that in America, a union
o fuckan lesbians, gays an coloured people –

cunts, thae jurnalists, as if we wisnae aa coloured –
huv got together wi academicks tae pruve that
whit's written in the papers ivry day
is jist as guid as whit fuckan Wullie Shakespeare
fucked us up wi at school. Jeez, fuckan marvelluz,
en't it, Jimmy? "Deconstructionists,"
they caa themsels. Appreciatiun at last,
eh Jimmy? "Deconstructionists." Whit the fuck…

Heh lassie, gieza a pint. Pit it oan the slate.
It cannae be closin time! It's no that late?

Maurice Lindsay

David Daiches

Flowers and Grocers

I took him for a drive in the car
When he was ninety-two, I less than half that.
He marvelled at the daffodils come round again,
And he still here. "Look," he said, "daffodils."
Is old age comforted by spring's return
Or do we see renewal as for nature
And not for us? He was alive for one more spring
At least. The cruelty of that indifference
Was felt by me and not by him.
I thought instead of how when we are gone
The round of life continues, grass and flowers and people,
Buds appear, grow fat, burst out,
People follow their daily rounds, intent
On their own trivialities. Couples court by the river
As though they were immortal and unique.
He broke into these thoughts with exclamation.
"Look," he said, reading a village shop-sign slowly,
"J Thomson, family grocer."
He smiled, and said again "J Thomson
Family grocer. He is a
Family grocer," he told me,
Earnest and pleased. "J Thomson, family grocer.
That's nice," he added, settling in his seat,
Touched by the ordinaryness.
I felt ashamed and moved. Why should this simple sign
Of undistinguished human dailiness
Have touched him so?

Ninety-two he was, not long for this world,
This world of daffodils and family grocers.
Now myself well past the Psalmist's span
Of seventy years I often think of this
And feel, surprisingly, a surge of love
For flowers and grocers everywhere.

Conductors

Tram conductors used to have machines
Strapped to their chests and issued tickets
With a musical 'ping', a penny one,
A tupenny or even a threepenny.
Progress has ended that.
On busses there are no conductors.
Give exact fare to the driver,
Who presses buttons, pushes levers,
And then re-starts the bus.
The old conductors fumbled for change
In leather bags worn over the shoulder
And counted out the coins into your palm,
Balancing like seamen as the tram lurched on.
Driving a tram was easy,
The rails carrying you where they led,
But the conductor,
Weighted and freighted with contraptions,
Choosing a ticket – each with its separate colour –
Fitting the proper space to his machine,
Punching the hole exactly,
Climbing upstairs and downstairs on the swaying tram,
Had a harder time.
Children went anywhere for a penny,
A yellow ticket. Red for a tupenny,
Blue for a threepenny.
Those chromatic journeys
Live in my memory like true adventures,
True adventure stories,
The conductor always the hero.

Streaks

Observation with extensive view
Said Dr Johnson, not numbering the streaks of the tulip.
Streaks of the tulip! What did he see
In his mind's eye when he used that phrase?
A tulip, streaked, stands sharply out

While all mankind from China to Peru
Blur in a chain or do a strip-the-willow
Or lose themselves in anthropology.
Short-sighted he was, streaked tulips
Were too difficult. Mankind's the thing:
The mind copes, not the eye. Just representation
Of general nature, he said.
Like
Parallel straight lines
Are straight lines
On the same plane
That never meet
However far
They are produced
In either direction.
But parallel lines do meet in the end
Our universe being what we know it is,
And just representation
Is unjust
And mankind
Is man-unkind.
And Dr Johnson
Wise, humane, sensible Dr Johnson,
Was really, as Boswell showed, unique.
Observation with intensive view
Showed all his streaks.
It is the streakiness that we remember.

Literary Criticism: Glasgow 1991

To be or not to fucking be,
That's the fucking question.
The silly cunt with the wee beard
Spouting fucking literature.
Even Rabbie fucking Burns
Wi' his fucking suppers
Is no for me.
Fuck off, the lot o' youse.

A highbrow version of the above

The curfew tolls the knell of fucking day,
The fucking herd winds slowly o'er the lea,
The fucking ploughman homewards wends his way,
And leaves the darkening fucking world to me.

David Daiches

Masters of Creative Writing

William Neill

We ought not to admire too slavishly all that is written by academic critics. The fate of that learned man who read a misprinted version of Yeats' poem which had "soldier Aristotle" for "solider Aristotle" and produced a note to the effect that Plato was playing marbles (tawse!) on Alexander's backside ought to be a horrid warning; so should Thynne's assumption that Henrysoun's "ochone" should really be read as "atone", an emendation which lacked both background research, linguistic knowledge and relevance to the context.

In an essay some years ago, Clive James wrote, on the subject of academic literary critics: "...there is the likelihood – some would say it is already an actuality – that the sheer volume of interpretation on offer will become a demand creating its own supply. The best route to success for a dull artist might be to create a work that needs interpretation. On the other hand the bright artist might go out of his way to avoid the attentions of the waiting owls."

Though vaguely disturbed by this, I selfishly assumed that the crisis would not come in my lifetime. However, a conversation, published recently in *Verse*, between Dana Gioia and Robert McPhillips, cured me of that illusion. "Dana Gioia...is unique among contemporary American poets. He does not have an MFA in Creative Writing." This is startling news indeed. It reinforces my prejudice that institutionalism of one kind or another has brought "the market for poetry" to a sorry condition. Gioia goes on to say that he is in favour of the New Formalism. Group-titles like this are the artistic equivalent to political parties. Nevertheless, I feel inclined to give three cheers for Mr Gioia. I have been practising formalism for years, aware that in our age this is a term of abuse.

Even before the invention of writing, it seems plain that formalism was the chief activity of poets. European poets, for about two thousand five hundred years, wrote thus. They continued to do so until about 1920 when free verse became more fashionable. Though once "competent versifiers" were common in poetry circles, nowadays they are an endangered species. There are, however, some younger poets who look on the past fifty years of chopped-prose cryptography with justifiable and commendable suspicion. Most "modern" poetry does not look or sound like poetry and is regarded as boring by many who enjoy other intelligent literary and dramatic works. There are also those who, addicted to what they euphemistically style "free verse", claim to have mastered all the classical forms in their not-so-distant youth. I discount light so conspicuously concealed under a bushel.

If literature is not in some way arresting, does not contain a reason for the reader to continue, it loses one of its main functions. Some "modern poetry", far from being arresting, is actually rebarbative. Blake's 'Tiger' is highly arresting but the "poems" of the opaque school just do not burn bright or even give the least spark of illumination. The tragedy is that opacity, which has virtually destroyed any wide readership for poetry, is welcomed by the annotating owls as raw material for their production line.

The usual defence of chopped-up prose is that it is "free verse", but *good* free verse, as Eliot pointed out, is not as free as many of its alleged exponents seem to think. It has an underlying rhythm which can be heard. Verse, (unlike poetry) has a fairly precise definition: "a line of metre, metrical composition" (Chambers); "Words arranged according to rules of prosody" (Oxford). These days it is common to thumb through poetry magazines seeking in vain for a single line which shows the most basic rhythm. Craftsmanship is a necessary foundation to art and those who oppose such a viewpoint are usually simply lazy or incompetent.

Easier, said Johnson, to say what poetry is not, than to define what it is. Few will quarrel with that. Prose, of course, is often poetic, but unless it has this underlying rhythm, a defining pattern, it remains prose however much it raises the hair on the nape of the neck. In discussing *poetry*, poetic prose is outside the remit. To count as *verse*, writing must have a recognisable rhythmic pattern.

Samuel Coleridge once remarked that poetry must do more than make good sense, but must at least do that. Most of the poets before 1920 made sense – even difficult ones like Donne. Coleridge does not mean the merest literal "sense", for *The Rime of the Ancient Mariner* and *Kubla Khan* do not function at that humble level. At first they may seem to do so, since they do not baffle the intelligent reader at the outset whereas a great many of the enigmas on offer today as poems surpass cypher in obscurity, since cypher can be decoded. It is sometimes argued that these offerings are an advance on the directness of Dunbar or Shakespeare, but that is not my opinion.

Masters' Degrees in Creative Writing indicate a drift away from the adage that poets are born, not made. Poetry until recently was created by a cross-section of society, not a group of cloistered scholars – departments of English Literature are comparative newcomers to universities. Neither Burns, Clare, nor Shakespeare attended universities, but nowadays there are some magazines whose credits read more like the staff of an institution of higher learning than a group of poets. I am not here denigrating such departments: educationally they do a fine job. But they are not a *sine qua non* of *literature*. However, they have a function other than teaching: research. In English departments, research usually takes the form of criticism or the production of modern literature. There is a natural tendency among academics to write for the attention of other academics. Some poets in universities will hope to kill two birds with one stone by writing what is likely to attract considerable academic comment, annotation and approval rather than general interest. It is difficult to write much annotation on what might be thought of as "simple poetry", even if simple poetry is not as simple as it seems. Most "simple" poetry accords with Coleridge's dictum and is not opaque to the intelligent reader at first

78

sight. The temptation of academics is to write poetry, not for the intelligent general reader but for the highly exclusive circle of fellow-academics.

I repeat that I am not here advocating the removal of Departments of English Literature. It is not merely an absurdity but an intellectual crime to exclude native cultures from universities founded in the territory which gave rise to such cultures. What I do plead is that twenty-five centuries of formal poetry may not be such an undesirable influence as some modern despisers of well-crafted stanzas seem to think and that formalism in contemporary poetry is still worthy of their attention. Without some sort of patterned structure there is no real poetry by definition. Verse is *patterned*, and prose may be poetic, but, and this cannot be said often enough, if it is not verse it is still *prose*. The idea of form does not exclude the invention of *new* patterns: what it does exclude is formlessness.

Dana Gioia says that he had to choose between "writing for the academic" and "writing for the common reader".He chose the latter rightly, because literature is not the private possession of cliques, however intellectually elevated. He points out that the common reader does not mean the unintelligent reader. It is notable that of the poets of past ages, many of the best were mediocre performers in the academic field. Wordsworth, Tennyson and Housman could have tried harder at Cambridge. Houseman actually failed to gain a degree (although they had to ask him back later since he knew more Latin than anyone there). Graves cavilled at orthodox exams. Thomas Hardy did not attend and wrote bitterly of Christminster/Oxbridge before deserting novels for formal verse of a highly individual kind.

If you ask the average intelligent person to quote poetry, the chances are that he will give you *formal poetry*, the memorable words. I am aware that this formal "poetry for the intelligent reader" is often despised by eager young post-grads with an eye to the ultimate accolade of a professorial chair, but they ought to recognise that their inner yearning springs from academic, not poetic, ambition. There is nothing wrong with this academic ambition provided their perceptions are not confused. Tramps, madmen, rebels, holy men, farmers, peasants and lords have all worn the poetic mantle in the past, but professors such as Housman appear very seldom in the poetic annals. They might also ponder the proposition that fake "layered poetry", whatever its capacity to con the cognoscenti, may be easier to make than good formal verse.

Many young poets, naturally curious about their chosen art, will take to reading essays on criticism. By all means let them do so, with the caveat that a great body of this is couched in language chosen to impress the reader with the alleged critic's mysterious lexis rather than to illuminate the work in question. It is often written by those who have never produced a stanza, let alone a poem, in their lives. Probably the only literary criticism worth reading is written by those whose primary interest is the writing of poems or novels. These pundits will convince the sensitive young poet that he ought to join a team, writing so that the great minds will take note of his work. But joining teams dedicated to any of these Movements: Moralists, Modernists, Structuralists, Deconstructionists, Organicists, Uncle-Tom-Cobbleyists, and writing for their critical approval, will simply muddy the spring from which poetry arises. A recent book, *Literary Theory and Poetry* (ed David Murray, Batsford), is a fairly typical example of the genre. All the many authors of the essays therein are lecturers in colleges or universities except one, who is a published poet. My advice to young poets would be, firstly: *read poems, not critical essays.* Secondly: *try to be unfashionable.* I am not here trying to start an Unfashionable Movement, but simply saying "make what *you* think is poetry". Furthermore, one of the greatest charms of literature lies in its sheer variety. We should pay no attention whatsoever to those non-poets who tell us that narrative poetry is dead or that craftsmanship of fine stanzas is old-fashioned. And bear in mind, poetry is often produced by those who have never read a word of literary criticism. It is sometimes produced by those who have been pooh-poohed by critics in their lifetime: Emily Dickinson, for instance. Always remember that much criticism is written by those who are seeking *academic* repute and are writing for the approval of professors, not poets.

If things proceed here as they apparently have done in America, a nightmare vision emerges. A state of affairs may arrive when Poetry (with a capital letter) will be totally under the control of academic institutions. The staff will write it, fellow academics will annotate it, rival professors will annotate the annotations. The university press (or those publishers daft enough to believe that academic=poet) will publish it. The Senate will criticise it. The Word-Hoard will be on The Syllabus. It will only contain words approved by the university. Writers of archaisms, borrowed words, neologisms will be discouraged, as well as any usage other than standard Poetic Lexis. All the Simpleminded Stuff (not requiring much exegesis) will be produced by Desktop Publishers and sold in batches of fifty.

I am of course aware that there are many academics in English Departments here who share the formalist viewpoint on poetry, who think that literature is for the intelligent reader and not merely the province of a Department. Let us hope that advancement in their careers comes rapidly, for at the moment the battle is going to those who would have all poets gain Firsts in Creative Writing followed by a doctorate in Annotation.

J S Mill's circular attempt to prove an objective value for poetry tends rather to the opposite conclusion: that poetry is what one likes it to be. My own inclinations side with the poets of two and a half millennia in that I like form, lyric, satire, and narrative. If I prefer these to a shapeless enjambment of arcane allusions owing more to a competitive scholarship than literature, you may think that my life and contacts have put me out of key with my time, but to me poetry is more a song than a puzzle.

William Neill

David Winwood

First Only One Person Possessed a Radio

then five hundred (and all tycoons
or of compatible elevation). But soon
the whole world buzzed, and aspirin
became a necessary adjunct to our diet.

The same with cars. Hiccough on wheels
became automobile: numbers with demands
for roads increased; its farts driving
away paradise from earth.

Television was followed head over heels
by computers and their compulsory
vision screens. Cybernetics steered us
toward total automation. Streetcars, trains,

buses, planes, all functioned without
human interference. Private cars still
followed orders, but set routes were credited
to their memory banks as a matter

of course. So one day we disappeared.
No car, streetcar, bus or plane that minded.
Repairs were already carried out unhumanly
and vandalism finally ceased.

The cat population collapsed. The rats
took over. But then, they'd always known
that the true strength of arithmetic
lies in the enjoyment of multiplication.

Food scarce at one place, they used
the automated vehicles. Soon a nomadic
lifestyle evolved which, combined with
leisure increased the species' intelligence.

Questions were asked. Grumbling started.
Why were these contraptions so damn
uncomfortable: the seats far too wide,
all windows too high up for looking out;

every safety belt ludicrously useless?
No account at all had been taken of
the creatures the vehicles were carrying.
"Now, this is very peculiar," the rats said.

"Something is wrong with creation."
And they stopped believing in God.

Beef

My grandmother was wide-built
and heavy. Would answer every insult
with a blast from a mouth that hardly
stopped talking. Once I fell asleep
on her lap and dreamt I possessed
all the wisdom she'd forgotten.

It didn't last. Now I remember her
in the living room, combing her hair,
checking in the mirror if that thin
grey-pale string was all. "It used
to be so long. And rich! I would coil
it twice around my head. People thought

it wasn't real." Seventeen I was and
school and speech training – to educate
away my accent – had left me without
an answer. I smelled the oil-stove
in her kitchen. She always simmered
the stringiest beef to an unbelievable

tenderness I have never tasted since.

Lovers and Friends
(for Katie)

Nobody believes in troubles, everybody
is wishing the water
not to ripple, for it to remain
the motionless mirror of happiness.
But the beast of the deep belches and farts
and ejects its young
like berries plopping from a blowpipe.
Ah, the waters of fate. You'd better believe the red
colour of the once glassy dark is for real.
Because suddenly from frayed
tempers the urge is woven
to flay all opponents alive. Foam on the mouths
of friends. Lovers refuse to bite back what they
swallowed only yesterday
We're all Thomases, probing
an Ocean's trough with a Chevvy's dipstick,
almightily surprised when the kraken
rises up and rips off our arm.

St Bernard

A stranger to winters of eight feet
of snow I was invited along as a joke.

Coming with us a dog like a barking sheep,
howling with joy in the car, ecstatic

when a sled was unloaded. barely in harness
he was off, first at a pedestrian canter

along the path; then, going down towards
the lake, he sunk out of sight in the snow;

came up four feet ahead and went down and up
with the sled following in his wake as

his waves rolled towards the ice's shore.
We drilled a hole with an auger and fished

for trout, those living, silver, peace symbols,
but all we caught was under the limit.

On our way back the dog's joy
still hadn't cooled, though the snow's crust

cracked menacingly through the dusk.
The St Bernard is dead now
and there's again another war on.

Only animals never get bored with life.

David Winwood

Kenneth Steven

My Land

The colour of a woman on her dying bed
A few straws of faded hair splayed on the pillow
Like streams with their rage of snow.
No red of rowan on the faint, half-open lips
Only an occasional breath, deep and broken
As the wind that covers the land.

I have wanted to leave such a long time
But this is my mother, I hold her hand.
In the fallen veins and the bloodless skin
There is the memory of freedom, of undying song
And the beat of a beautiful drum.

Island of Lewis

As I was coming back through Gravir
Against the mist, an old woman stopped me
Eyes large as the sky
Hands like a hillside winding with streams
And she asked, Where are you from?
I thought of all the nowhere towns
I had eaten, slept, talked, passed
The vague places on a wandered map
And her hands made of home
The voice stronger than her back with Gaelic
Her roots where my soil was dead.

Potato Picking

A spun splitting of mud
The tractor goes asthmatically on, smoking
And the baskets skud down, backs bend
The head bloods, a blush of gold
Rushes the skirts of trees.

The tinkers are ahead
Ingrained with tide-marks of deft generations
Their language hot as whisky.
Eyes that sift faces, the fleet of horses
Faster than a buttoned world.

We drop to eat, raucous as crows;
The sun bends down river in oils
Flocks of gabbling swan-water reach the falls.
We lie under sky as young, as free
As the red hawks that wink in heaven.

Wolves

Stalactites in a caved mouth
Cry the land to fossil.
Eyes made of luminous moon
Amber of the trees first hunters felled.

They pad the winter's fear
Holding the horizon to ransom
The lampoon of upraised howl
Grey-echoed over homeless miles
To ring like standing stones the wind.

Last tooth of the wild
Cutting the north to jagged bone.

The Fishing

There is a gap in the hills
And we could have filled our pockets
With lines and red-cold hands
A fire in our eyes already.

This is the moorland where time is dead
In the empty sockets lochs blow
And over bones the sharp crag of heather
A deer standing guard on the wind.

In the evening a moon unfolds her skirts
On the low sleep of the land
And an owl with a limp in the thick wings
Blinks over quartz miles.

Will you come then, Malcolm
Or is it too late now? Your hands with a daughter
And mine buried and broken
By the weight of a city.

Kenneth Steven

George Gunn

Red

The red-faced dead who are not yet dead
but are pending, rise up like hungry seals
after fish in the early spring evening
in the mouth of a sea loch, preparing
for this apocalypse & what is there to offer
a line of expectants duly filing past
the open fast-food hatch of delirium history
or my mouth or their boot, a leather
of teeth & philosophy, jambokked
into the korral of one's own country
or how better to put it as we chat up the reaper
how much blood can we spill into our veins
& how long can we sustain a civil war
in our imagination, stop them in the street
& ask them what they think as they dream
in a long dead Hebrew of fish suppers
& the fatal last drink & the colour is still red

Stromness

The blue sea & the green islands
are waiting in the mid-day
of their time, the paved
street shapes the town
& the air is full of prawn husk
& the fat smell of a morning's baking
feeds the rain-soaked fishing boats
as they harbour in their tang
By sea we came here once
younger then in our substance
fresher in our longings
than the tied & fast lieutenants
of other people's beating geographies
We came here with our dream

ii

The quiet bird sings
a barn owl in a green
hayfield, mouse
eager eyes a chronicle
of hunting, I longed
through this like a rainshower
as the pillars of light
held Hoy to the world
I thought of us there
stone-collecting, walking
a bright duo in a flagstone bothan
I looked home and saw
the angels of circumstance
flying over Dunnet Head

Whins

To be so spiky & smell of coconut
so bizarre, you will not
let me touch you
like my love you are
an army upon the hillside
before the war, waiting
but I have no command for you
nothing inside me save
for what you put there
a sea of yellow
in a darkening world

The Russian Revolution – Take Two

Going to Dundee on a beautiful summer afternoon
in a long-awaited August of heat

meal factories & trees' blossom
like the pulsating flesh of horses

the clouds are clapping the sky
like the gloved jokes in a comedian's

azure repertoire & my mind fixes
like a TV screen onto a man on a tank

& how he is everybody's new darling
but he's not mine: to me he's

a dangerous demagogue in an uncertain time
when fresh dictators are waiting to come on

like actors from the wings & I wish
that they did have wings & that they could fly

over the rolling fertile plains of Angus
where the barley & wheat & oats

are queueing up to be the colour of honey
& it will be cut as will

all dicators in the black cropping
before the light of morning where ideas

are baked in the oven of need
I say, the harvest has begun

George Gunn

The Ceilidh House

The High Street wis yince a hub o music, poetry an' talk.
The Ceilidh House pits back that tradeetioun.
Folk nichts – poetry nichts – an aye-bidan come-aa-ye

ilka nicht o the week a new stramash!

Cleik yer pals in fur a pint or a dram. Ye'll hae a waarm walcome.

Eldritch neuks and crannies fur smaa foregaitherings
Cellar haa fur middlin-scale occasiouns

The Ceilidh House, 9 Hunter Square, Edinburgh EH1 1QW
Heid Wanger: Cy Laurie
Tel 031-220 1550

Reviews

A Misunderstood Monster?

Poor Things, Alasdair Gray, Bloomsbury, £14.99

In a self-written blurb for this book, Alasdair Gray says his publisher "suspects it will be his most popular novel". Whether Bloomsbury ever made such a statement I have no idea, but it could well turn out to be true. The book is written in a clear style, or a series of clear styles; it is entertainingly and swiftly readable; it has at its core a variation of an earlier, almost mythically well-known story, Mary Shelley's *Frankenstein*; and it has many eye-catching illustrations, from Gray himself, from Gray 'after' the Scottish Victorian etcher William Strang, from Gray's (no relation, as they say) *Anatomy*, and from anonymous Victorian book-illustrations. If, at a second reading, certain doubts make themselves felt, these affect the book's depth, but not its readability.

The novel unfolds its tale almost entirely through reminiscences and letters, and is wrapped around by an authorial introduction giving supposedly circumstantial details of how the facts behind the story were discovered, and an authorial epilogue of "notes critical and historical" which similarly mingles information and disinformation in typically deadpan style. Whether all this, coupled with the book's parodies of both Victorian fictional dialogue and Victorian melodramatic plotting, to say nothing of the fact that the story is told twice, once in a science-fiction mode and once giving naturalistic explanations, implies a post-modern playfulness and teasing of the reader, there are clearly also strong backward glances at technique used by Scott and Hogg, if one wants to think of it as a 'Scottish' novel.

Godwin Bysshe Baxter is an ugly but benevolent surgeon who as his name tells us is a prophet like William Godwin (Mary Shelley's father) and a creator of life (indeed he is familiarly called God) like the hero of Mary Shelley's novel. Unlike Dr Frankenstein however, he reanimates an actual body, and does so in an original way which is part of the didactic plan of the book, implanting the brain of her nine-month foetus into the head of a young woman who had drowned herself in the Clyde. Bella Baxter becomes the heroine of the book, and after various erotic and melodramatic adventures marries the rather fashionless Dr Archibald McCandless who tells her story, ending up herself as nurse and doctor. She begins as a physically attractive girl (with telltale scars in certain places), wide-eyed and innocent as her child's brain learns to cope with the adult experience her body cannot but give her. Her language at first stutters in monosyllables ("Hell low Miss terr Candle") but soon burgeons into joyful synonyms and quotations as she picks up a range of expression through reading and talking ("I am taking Candle for a walk saunter stroll dawdle trot canter short gallop and circum-ambu-*lation*"). She is clearly a free spirit, and the most entertaining part of the book, recounted first in 'Wedderburn's Letter' and then in 'Bella Baxter's Letter', tells how she elopes with Duncan Wedderburn, a "plausible, unscrupulous, lecherous lawyer", drags him over Europe and the Middle East, tires him out with her relentless sexual vitality, and eventually drives the shattered creature totally mad. Near-farcical scenes are interspersed with philosophical disquisitions, Peacock-style, on the state of the world, which are designed to help Bella search for a fourth, better way than foolish innocence, callous optimism or desperate cynicism. She is strong in herself, but has to learn how to use her "free intelligence to plan better ways of doing things", beginning at an interpersonal level but perhaps feeding a helpful and healing leaven out through society, not unlike the heroine of *Middlemarch*. She is galvanised out of any remaining tatters of innocence and ignorance by one incident which is crucial to the effect of the novel. During her travels, she is sitting on a veranda in Alexandria, watching Egyptian beggars touting for coins down below, under the whips of overseers. When she sees a thin one-eyed girl holding a blind baby in one arm and begging with the other, she tries to rescue them and take them back to Britain but is stopped from doing so and told in capital letters YOU CAN DO NO GOOD. Her horror and pity are intensified by

GOOD. Her horror and pity are intensified by thoughts of her own lost daughter, but Gray does not allow this to detract from the social issue, the 'vile' suggestion that it is impossible to do anything about the cruelties and injustices of society. This is a theme that Gray always warms to, and one blesses him for it. As Bella says:

> I clenched my teeth and fists to stop them biting and scratching these clever men who want no care for the helpless sick small, who use religions and politics to stay comfortably superior to all that pain: who make religions and politics, excuses to spread misery with fire and sword and how could I stop all this? I did not know what to do.

Bella's agonised reaction to the Alexandria incident is shown graphically by six 'facsimile' pages of her letter, scrawled and tearsplotched, a few vowelless words reduced to near-incomprehensibility, a "catastrophic reversion to an earlier phase" as McCandless describes it, but spelt out by Baxter as:

> no no no no no no no no no, help blind baby, poor little girl help both, trampled no no no no no no no no no no no no no no no no no no, no where my daughter, no help for blind babies poor little girls

The use of a visual effect, whether through drawings or through typography, links this passage to the moment of McLeish's self-redemption near the end of *1982, Janine*, when his tears come pouring through a column of *Ach*'s, ending with the "Ach poor children, poor children" which is so like the tenor of *Poor Things*. I do not find *Poor Things* so moving, however. Partly this is because Gray, in his guise as Victorian narrator and mentor, has to explain painstakingly that the six pages have been "printed by a photogravure process which exactly reproduces the blurring caused by tear stains, but does not show the pressure of pen strokes which often ripped right through the paper". The conscious didacticism of a fiction which is really nearer fable than novel does tend to cool the emotional impact, even though in the quoted passage it is meant to reinforce it. I think also we remember that McLeish is an adult with recognisable human problems, whereas Bella is a person with (literally) a child's brain, not naturally human though full of good qualities. This

argument, however, is not the full story, since we are far more strongly moved by Dr Frankenstein's creation in Mary Shelley's novel: the 'monster', like Bella, is a fabrication, but rouses intense sympathy as well as awe and terror in the reader, and forces thought into areas of deeper import, speculation and questioning than the sociopolitical concerns of *Poor Things*. Perhaps the comparison is unfair; *Frankenstein* is a tragedy, *Poor Things* is a comedy. I would not quarrel with Philip Hensler, one of the judges on the *Guardian*, which awarded the book that newspaper's prize for contemporary fiction, when he called it "as irresistible as cream cake, and as nourishing as lentils". The lentils of good doctrine are indeed wholesome. But the grandeur of *Lanark*, and the sharp human drama of *1982, Janine*, are not here matched on their own level. What we have is hugely enjoyable and often instructive, a story set up in such a way that the reader's delight in documentary and pseudo-documentary devices is almost taken for granted, since the actual narrative line is relatively thin, but where pleasure is never far away, nor on the other hand our sense of the author's sighs and groans over "the way we live now".   *Edwin Morgan*

Listening for Ancestral Voices

Essequibo, Ian McDonald, Peterloo Poets £6.95; *The Natal Papers of 'John Ross'*, Charles Rawdon Maclean (ed Stephen Gray), University of Natal Press, special order; *Collected Poems*, Les Murray, £18.95; *Translations from the Natural World*, Les Murray, £6.95, both Carcanet

Is there an essential 'Scottishness' somehow transmitted genetically to the many millions overseas whose Scottish names proclaim ancestry? If so, where does that leave the people important and loved in present day Scotland whose forebears arrived recently from Italy, Scandinavia, Poland? To pose these rhetorical questions at all is to suggest the answer that 'Scotland' is remade in every generation, and that any humane and reasonable person should eschew talk about eternal Scottish ethnicity which threatens incomers.

When one reads that Ian McDonald is

"Trinidadian by birth, Guyanese by adoption... West Indian by conviction," one supposes that he might be one of the many black Caribbeans whose slave ancestors acquired surnames from their Scottish owners. Discovering that he is white encourages one to look out in his new book of poems for Scottish references. Fruitless. Stylistically, the writer I'm most often reminded of is that wonderful Welshman, Edward Thomas. McDonald's poems about the river and forest life of Guyana are haunted by consciousness of the land's original inhabitants. 'Amerindian' opens the book. "I think of woodskins, I think/ of quick arrows." 'Carib Bones' confronts the militant, proud traditions of old survivors "scratching withered genitals". But this consistently impressive and enjoyable book, in which poor people are transfigured by the awesomely rich environment of the land once thought to be 'El Dorado', never once hints at Gaelic analogies.

In contrast, for Les Murray, now generally acknowledged to be one of the most important poets using any form of English, Scottish antecedents are insistent. In an 'Elegy for Angus Macdonald' he pays tribute to a scholar preserving Gaelic tradition. "Teacher of my heart, you'll not approve/ my making this in the conqueror's language." But this Macdonald died in Sydney, NSW, and Murray is an Australian nationalist:

Now, in the new lands, everyone's Ethnic and we too, the Scots Australians, who've been henchmen of much in our self-loss may recover ourselves, and put off oppression.

Exiled Gaels were complicit in the massacre of aborigines: yet the concept of 'clan', emphasised in a long and moving poem about the early death of Murray's mother, has its place in the building of a new nation. In his brilliant 'Late Snow in Edinburgh', the "visitor-descendant", watching the "multiplying whiteness" dissolve suddenly, wryly regrets that there will be no miracle here to mark Anzac Day tomorrow, only "Hughie Spring,/ the droll ploughman, up from the Borders."

In 'Equinoctial Gales at Hawthornden Castle' in his latest book, *Translations from the Natural World*, Murray adjusts a tradition of the Bruce to suit his own current preoccu-

pation with inarticulate creatures:

Allegedly beneath its steeps wound the deep pict
cave where the Bruce once lay, licked,
watching a bob spider cast, time on time,
it's whole self after the slant rhyme
of purchase needed to stay its transverse
then radial map of the universe
and all the tiny mixed krill that
too would jewel the king as he burst out.

For the distinguished South African poet Stephen Gray, the point of setting the record straight about 'John Ross' is to assist in the construction of a new multiracial national identity. 'John Ross' *was* 'John' because he was a 'Jack Tar' - to his patron the great Zulu King, 'Jackabo'. His red hair made him Gaelic 'Ross'. His real name was Charles Maclean (1815–1880). Born the son of a naval officer in Fraserburgh, he was barely ten when shipwrecked on the African coast at the place called 'Port Natal' by Europeans. Later, faulty memory or a motive to do with his career made him add a couple of years to his age. This contributes one of many elements of uncertainly to the conflict between his testimony about his three years as one of a small group of stranded whites in the realm of the 'Emperor' Shaka and those of other Britons on that coast at that time.

White South African historians neglected his memoirs serialised in the *Nautical Magazine* of London a quarter of a century after he left Natal. They developed for their own ends a legend of 'John Ross' as the wee boy who made a remarkable march to Portuguese-held Deiagoa Bay, alone save for a 'savage' escort, to get 'necessaries' for his forlorn shipmates. In fact, he did so under the protection of Shaka, who had taken him into his court, at first as pet, later as trusted upper servant and counsellor. But this conflicts with the Myth of Shaka as the blood-crazy 'Black Napoleon'. As recently as 1987, an SABC TV serial about 'Ross' presented him as a fabulous exemplar of natural white superiority in a domain of evil and peril. Yet Maclean repeatedly emphasised his gratitude to the Zulus who had fed and defended him in his vulnerable childhood, and his urgent concern that the whites who, when he wrote, had mastered Natal, should treat his old friends with respect and justice.

Becoming in due course a merchant captain

plying the route between Britain and the West Indies, Maclean never ceased to believe that black people were his equals. In 1846 he provoked a minor diplomatic incident when the North Carolina authorities demanded, according to local law, that his black crewmen should be jailed until his ship was ready to sail: he retorted that he would shoot his cannon at any posse which tried to seize them. In his last years, Maclean turned colonial official on St. Lucia, protecting the rights of the island's black people as 'stipendiary magistrate'. So he has a rather significant place in the history of the tiny nation now belaurelled through Walcott's poems and Nobel Prize. Gray's patient pioneering researches have retrieved a man whose Scottish birth became a marginal fact in a remarkable life. When we say we're all 'Jock Tamson's Bairns' we should always remember that Jock himself was of mixed ancestry, and the culture of our own country has come, like that of the Caribbean, from across oceans. *Angus Calder*

Auld Sangs Dirl Again

A Biography of Robert Burns, James Mackay, Mainstream, £20; *Alias MacAilias*, Hamish Henderson, £12.95; *The Sang's the Thing*, ed Sheila Douglas, £9.95, both Polygon; *One Singer One Song*, Ewan McVicar, Glasgow City Libraries, £4.99

An interesting and varied selection of volumes here, all of strong interest to the lover of Scottish song. The first, James Mackay's scholarly and balanced *A Biography of Robert Burns*, is an excellent addition to the Burns canon, and a long overdue corrective to the works of hagiography and demonology which have been served up since the poet's death. The research has been meticulous, and Mackay, unlike many other Burns chroniclers, has taken nothing for granted. Already fully conversant with the poems, songs and letters – his *The Complete Works of Robert Burns* (1986) and *The Complete Letters of Robert Burns* (1987) are required reading for any serious Burns enthusiast – Mackay has sought out primary sources, checked for cross-references wherever possible, and examined the work of his predecessors in the field thoroughly and critically. The result is a book which will become *the* standard text and reference.

To those whose interest in Burns is prurient, who prefer to see him as a drunken, debauched womaniser, seeking to excuse their own weaknesses or justify their self-righteousness by picking over salacious details, this volume will come as a disappointment. Mackay gathers the evidence, considers it with care, and presents us with a sympathetic but unsentimental account of the life of a man who, if no saint, was certainly not the irresponsible rake that many have carelessly assumed him to be. Looking at proof rather than fable, three, and possibly four, illegitimate daughters were born. Interestingly, he did intend to marry Elizabeth Paton, mother of 'dear-bought Bess', when she became pregnant, but was dissuaded by his brother Gilbert and his sisters. Jean Armour bore him nine children, but in the context of the times and the infant mortality rate, this was by no means unusual.

The romantic and much-mythologised 'Highland Mary' is convincingly identified as one Margaret Campbell, although we still know little of her relationship with the bard, whether she bore him a child, or the manner of her death. Contrary to reports elsewhere, Mackay has not advocated the grisly and profane notion that there should be DNA testing of the remains in Greenock Cemetery: he merely mentions that it is technically feasable.

As Mackay correctly points out, a man habitually the worse for drink could never have sustained the workload that Robert Burns did during the Ellisland and Dumfries years. Apart from his strenuous duties as exciseman, and the farm work, he was at this point collecting and writing songs for both James Johnson, the honest and decent compiler of *The Scots Musical Museum*, and the self-satisfied George Thomson who not only took considerable unpoetic license with the marvellous material Burns sent him, but also bears a large share of blame for subsequent denigration of the poet's character. His ill-judged and gratuitous reference in an obituary report reads: "The public, to whose amusement he greatly contributed, will learn with regret that his extraordinary endowments were accompanied with frailties which rendered them useless to himself and his family." One has only to read James Mackay's admirable account to understand how Burns worried for the future of his wife and children and how desperately he tried to improve his financial prospects. In these circumstances it may seem extraordinary that he sought no payment for his work for Johnson and Thomson but, like many before and since, he had an almost sacred regard for the songs of his native land.

Hamish Henderson, whose collection of essays and reviews *Alias MacAlias* is at long last with us, is another who has devoted much of his life, huge talent, and commendable energy to the Scottish folk tradition. This treasure-store of a book covers not the whole broad sweep of Hamish's interests – this would require a fair-sized library – but a goodly selection of those things which are his passion: songs, folklore, literature and people. As is only to be expected in a work that covers more than forty years of writing and broadcasting there are some repetitions, but, in the main, these are important and fundamental points and they reaffirm rather than jar.

And it is the people who shine forth in this book. Jeannie Robertson, Jimmie MacBeath, Willie Scott, Duncan Williamson and a dozen more are drawn not with the dry objectivity of the academic but with the warm feeling of a man, a man of great intellect to be sure, but also a man of deep human understanding. He can give a clear-eyed but compassionate account of 'Germany in Defeat' dating from 1948, write a review of the prose of Garcia Lorca which brings a lump to the throat and, in 'MacGonagall the What', give that adopted Dundonian what is probably the fairest appraisal, graced with humour and affection, that he has ever had.

When writing of his work in collecting songs Hamish wonderfully conveys the sense of excitement, the delicious anticipatory tingle, and the sheer thrill of coming across a singer or a song fresh to your ears. His account, twice told (and why not?), of the meeting of Willie Scott and Willie Mitchell at Blairgowrie is a delight. It was a great night's singing and Willie Scott got from Willie Mitchell the words of 'Callieburn' which he later famously sang, but to a tune transformed from what he had heard. The oral tradition is indeed a magical thing!

My favourite quote comes in a 1955 Saltire Review essay 'Enemies of Folksong' where those who assume that everything worth retaining is already safely and tidily presented in a book of Scottish Song are being corrected:

> 'But what on earth are you going to do with all this stuff once you have collected it?' comes a parting shot from the opposing camp. The answer is: give it back to the Scottish people who made it.

Absolutely, and I hope the School of Scottish Studies takes note! A song is a living thing and it is cruel to lock it away from its natural home which is in the heart and voice of a singer.

The stout hearts and sturdy voices of 28 Lowland singers, fisherfolk and farmhands, travellers and townies, shine through *The Sang's the Thing*, edited by Sheila Douglas. Here we have the words and music of 58 songs ranging from Jane Turriff's classic variant of 'Barbary Allen' to Jim Brown's tongue-in-cheek 'Ball-Shy Boy From Moscow', along with the stories of those who sang them.

In most cases, the singers are speaking for themselves: Dr Douglas has transcribed the Lowland tongues with skill. In this valuable addition to Scottish history and song, the extraordinary courage, decency and resilience of 'ordinary' people stands revealed, nowhere more strongly than in Barbara Findlay's moving evocation of her father, Willie Barclay.

While many of the songs in Sheila's book came from country folk, Ewan McVicar's *One Singer One Song* concentrates on songs and singers with a Glasgow connection, with, of course, one song from each, and a commentary laced with Ewan's own virtuoso doggerel. There are some odd choices, like the slight 'Wee Gallus Bloke' to represent a great ballad singer like Gordeanna McCulloch, but on the whole it's a good and fun collection.

The only song to appear in both books is Norman Buchan's 'Auchengeich Disaster'. 'The Shipyard's Apprentice' has its lyrics ascribed by McVicar entirely to Archie Fisher but, to his last days, Norman, an honourable man, averred that he co-wrote it. That is also the recollection of Janey Buchan and of Gordeanna McCulloch who was involved in the BBC *Landmark* series from whence it came.

Sheena Wellington

Devolving History

Andrew Fletcher and the Treaty of Union, Paul H Scott, John Donald, £25; *The Dundas Despotism,* Michael Fry, Edinburgh University Press, £18.95; *The Manufacture of Scottish History,* ed Ian Donnachie and Christopher Whatley, Polygon, £8.95

On your left, as you enter the Bank of Scotland on the Mound, is a large, full-length Raeburn portrait of Henry Dundas, first viscount Melville, one of the bank's original governors. He wears state robes and has a slightly quizzical look in his eyes, as if hoping that the pose will not take up too much of his valuable time. The portrait graces the cover of Michael Fry's *The Dundas Despotism.* Dundas, as Fry convincingly argues, was very much a man of the Enlightenment, not least in his attempts to remove legal restrictions against Catholics in Scotland. In this endeavour he was defeated by bigots of all classes, including the Edinburgh mob, but he was otherwise very rarely on the losing side.

Andrew Fletcher of Saltoun lived a couple of generations before Dundas, but he was certainly a precursor of the Enlightenment, not least in his prescient political works. The greatest of these is *An Account of a Conversation* (1704), a Platonic dialogue which debates the arguments for and against the forthcoming Union. His only contemporary rival in this genre was Bishop Berkeley. As for the cover portrait of Fletcher (after William Aikman), it suggests a man of stern principles ready, nevertheless, to engage in civilised discussion.

A prototype Whig, and therefore no Jacobite, Fletcher opposed the Treaty of Union, and on principles more universal than those of the Jacobites. Dundas, on the other hand, very much a Tory, embraced the Union and worked brilliantly within its limits to benefit Scots from all walks of life. From the time he was appointed Lord Advocate for Scotland in 1775 to his impeachment for financial impropriety in 1805, Dundas was the most powerful man in Scotland. He "managed" most of the MPs, and was close to the Prime Minister, Pitt the younger. He also held a number of important ministerial posts, including Treasurer of

the Navy and Secretary of State for War. His reputation plummeted in the Victorian period however, and he came to be regarded as a scion of the corrupt system of rotten boroughs and blatant parliamentary patronage.

Andrew Fletcher's reputation, by contrast, increased despite his political failure in preventing an "incorporating Union" between England and Scotland. Scott's book is preoccupied, quite naturally, with how Scotland lost her last vestige of independence with the Treaty of Union. As a result, he has been damned with faint praise by Allan Massie in *The Times Literary Supplement* for writing "an interesting but partisan book" and supposedly being "more concerned to make a case than to exercise the impartiality proper to a historian." Since Scott's focus is on how Fletcher was affected not only by the Treaty of Union, but also his role in British politics since the "Glorious Revolution", his scope is far from narrow; no biographer of Fletcher, moreover, could avoid partisanship of some sort. Scott emphasises that Fletcher was not against Union as such, but against an *incorporating* Union. He had no objection to a *federal* Union, where England and Scotland would have been equal partners, but Massie, despite mentioning the difficulties some Thatcherites have with the word "federal" in relation to the European Community, conveniently ignores this crucial aspect of Fletcher's political position. Scott, in any case, is particularly good at describing the political debates and byzantine manoeuvres which preceded the Treaty of Union, and is highly perceptive in his analysis of Fletcher's lucid political pamphlets.

Timely and illuminating, *Andrew Fletcher and the Treaty of Union* may be partisan in its objectives, but is impartial in its sifting of evidence. It also usefully includes the articles of the Treaty of Union in an appendix for the reader to examine. A truly biased account of the Treaty of Union for Massie to consider would be Daniel Defoe's *The History of the Union of Great Britain* which, as Scott points out, "makes no reference to Fletcher at all."

Scott evidently admires his chosen political hero: the same is also true of Michael Fry, though Dundas seems altogether less heroic than Fletcher of Saltoun. He emerges as an authoritarian, especially in his treatment of alleged Jacobin dissidents in Scotland (during wartime, lest we forget); but if a despot, at least he was an enlightened one. Political stability in which Scottish civil society could flourish seems to have been his main political goal as Fry portrays him. He was no ideologue – in this he was not dissimilar to David Hume or Adam Smith – but a pragmatist. His head was in Westminster, his heart in Scotland.

He was also a grand strategist of the British Empire. He strengthened Britain's hold on India, while his seizure of the Cape from the Dutch in order to thwart Napoleon's global ambitions still has fateful consequences in South Africa today. He vigorously preferred the Empire to be a trading enterprise rather than a colonial one: later, Victorian, Empire-builders unfortunately had other ideas.

Above all, Dundas comes across as a certain kind of indispensable politician who is all too often misunderstood by those who fail to recognise the nature of politics, and how political realities operate. This is how Fry puts it, eloquently comparing Dundas to two of his most famous political colleagues:

> Politics certainly has to find room for deep thinkers, such as, in this age, Edmund Burke. It must also find room for public spirit and high integrity, of the sort that William Pitt the younger exemplified. But politics would scarcely be possible at all without the practical men, those who appreciate that the choice usually lies between two evils, who strike the bargains and push through the measures that make political systems work, and who take the punishment when they do not. Without them the deep thought, public spirit and high integrity would go for nothing. Dundas was one of these.

Fry's reassessment of Dundas could not be better summed up. A less forceful, but equally powerful figure, was his son Robert, second viscount Melville, whose political career Fry also covers. Robert continued his family's ascendancy in Scottish politics until the triumph of the Whigs in 1830.

Fry has also contributed a stimulating essay, 'The Whig Interpretation of Scottish History' in *The Manufacture of Scottish History*. He argues that Whig historians like H T Buckle tended to downgrade Scottish *political* history on the grounds that, as W L Mathiesson,

another Whig historian put it, Scotland's "political history had ended with the abolition of the Scottish representative system in 1832." Whig historians, according to Fry, considered Scottish political affairs to be beneficially subordinated to Westminster. Only social history therefore mattered; moreover, a sentimental kind of social history along the lines of the kailyard school in literature.

The Dundas Despotism and *Andrew Fletcher and the Treaty of Union* are both important contributions to the revision of Scottish political history. The essays in *The Manufacture of Scottish History*, varied and consistently entertaining to read, remind us that however important political history may be, in the House of History there are many mansions, *pace* Fry, in the aforementioned contribution, when he declares with sarcastic disapproval: "Hence we in Scotland too must compete in dredging the lower depths of history from below, and in hauling up out of oblivion all the submerged groups: women, ethnic minorities, sexual deviants, criminals and lunatics." As the rest of the essay is so persuasive and incisive, this outburst can only be charitably attributed to a surfeit of polemical high spirits. Joy Hendry's essay on 'Women's History in Scotland', Ian Donnachie on 'The Enterprising Scot', Charles Withers on 'The Historical Creation of the Scottish Highlands', and George Rosie on 'Museumry and the Heritage Industry' all demonstrate that political realities are often shot through with myths and preconceptions, and therefore not quite as clear-cut as politically conservative historians like Fry might recognise.

As for Angus Calder's highly suggestive essay 'The Enlightenment', it demonstrates how inadequate *merely* political history can be in exploring Scotland's contribution to that great European intellectual ferment, even failing to illuminate such a great mind as David Hume, or "how Hume was Scottish and only Scotland could have produced Hume." What seems beyond dispute, however, is that all three books make crucial contributions to devolving Scottish history from too exclusive a focus on the British state.

Mario Relich

Theatre Roundup

Imagine a play featuring Elaine C Smith, Russell Hunter, Una McLean and Robbie Coltrane… and that was just the audience. On stage there was Gerard Kelly, Andy Gray and David Hayman and a supporting cast of young Scottish acting talent too numerous to list. The event – and it did seem like an event – was Rain Dog's revival of John Byrne's *Still Life*, the third instalment in the celebrated *Slab Boys* trilogy, which reunited the original cast of ten years ago. And just as the play propels the loveable rogues from the Paisley carpet factory forward in time away from the idealism of youth and into the cynicism born of cold experience, so this production seemed to mark the end of a chapter in Scottish theatre history. Kelly, Gray and Hayman are no longer the aspiring young hopefuls, but the familiar faces of the establishment.

The inspired idea behind Caroline Paterson's production was to merge elements of *The Slab Boys* and *Cuttin' a Rug* into *Still Life*. Now when Hayman's Phil McCann and Kelly's Spanky Farrell swapped anecdotes, their stories emerged ghost-like from around the gravestones. It was a lot to squeeze into the Arches stage, but the overall effect was to enrich the script, to make it less of a sequel and more of a fully-written play in its own right; to keep it funny, but also to beef up the lingering atmosphere of melancholy and loss.

It was a season of star names. Soon after Rain Dog's celebrity line-up came Tom Courtenay at the Traverse, Rupert Everett at The Citizens', Gregor Fisher as Rab C Nesbitt on tour, Elaine C Smith in Willy Russell's *Shirley Valentine* and Dorothy Paul in her own *That's Her Again*. That four of these were one-person shows (not counting the guy lying on the bed and Dave Anderson occasionally sticking his head round the door in the excellent Nesbitt show) might say something about the state of theatre economics, but in none of the cases did it seem like the audience was being sold short.

Moscow Stations, directed by Ian Brown at Edinburgh's Traverse Theatre, was more an opportunity for Tom Courtenay to give a bravura performance than an example of a great play. Stephen Mulrine's version of Venedikt Yerofeev's cult novel saw Courtenay meandering from story to story, station to station, as the central character, an intellectual drunk, making his inebriated way through the Moscow underground. The play was a homage to the heroism of those whose response to the oppression of the Soviet system was to pour themselves a kind of alcoholic escape route, and the skill of Mulrine's adaptation was in its tendency to blur in and out of focus making it seem like we, the audience, were drunk as well. Courtenay lived his lines with freshness and spontaneity, tweaking out rhythmical patterns with a rare assuredness, deftly handling the audience's responses and swinging through his lines with rooted control.

Another one-man show, Barry Collins' *Judgement*, which Giles Havergal directed and starred in at the Citizens', was a trimmed-down version of the original. Havergal's interpretation was no less powerful as he played the cool, moderated prisoner of war making his defence for eating his fellow inmates in order to survive, his detached, unshowy delivery drawing us into its edgy ethical debate. No doubt Havergal had one eye to the bank-balance when he programmed such an economical show, but typically there was no compromise in artistic standards.

Believing strongly in team spirit, the Citz refuses to play along with the London star system – big names like Rupert Everett are listed on the press release like any other actor. The Citz leaves any trumpet-blowing to others, and lets its reputation stand or fall on the strength of its artistic output alone. Appearing as Lord Henry Wotton in Philip Prowse's adaptation of *A Picture of Dorian Gray*, Everett played with characteristic camp languor and disdain in an assured performance opposite Henry Ian Cusick's Dorian Gray. Philip Prowse's lush design – some felt too lush – added some outrageous touches to the story (Dorian poses for his portrait as a crucified Christ) and gave the whole piece a lavish air.

Ian Wooldridge began his last season as Artistic Director of the Royal Lyceum with Juliet Cadzow delivering a neat balance of Morningside severity and free-thinking libertarianism in *The Prime of Miss Jean Brodie*. Guest director Caroline Hall came up with a slick, straightforward production, but was inevitably limited by the adaptation's forced framing device which did little justice to the subtleties of Muriel Spark's original.

Richard Barron took his turn next, directing Arthur Miller's *The Price*: a good opportunity to see this infrequently-performed family drama about deception, sacrifice and compromise. The production's limitation – and it's a difficult one to surmount – is that the actors weren't able to bring the physical and emotional weight that Miller's lived-in characters require. As a result it was difficult to believe that these people had been through thirty years of anger, deceit and confusion.

Hugh Hodgart had no weighty themes to deal with when he came to directing Goldoni's *Mirandolina*, and produced a thoroughly silly, totally trivial and highly enjoyable version that refused to take itself seriously. A cheery, grinning Fiona Bell led the company (including live goat) through this early feminist romp in which male conceit and self-indulgence is lampooned and the hard-nosed wit and invention of the young Mirandolina is celebrated.

Robin Peoples at the Brunton Theatre ran through a short season of plays by women. Beginning with *Love But Her*, Lara Jane Bunting's lyrical tribute to the life of Jean Armour, the long-suffering wife of Robert Burns, the season moved on to a rewritten revival of Liz Lochhead's *The Big Picture*, a nostalgic ode to growing up in a dead-end small-town, and finished on a particularly successful note with an adaptation of *84 Charing Cross Road*, which worked despite being based almost entirely on exchanged letters, thanks to convincing and well-moderated performances from Vivienne Brown and Robert Paterson.

Hamish Glen proved the promise of his debut autumn season at Dundee Rep, following up Gerry Mulgrew's inventive, economical and timely production of *Hard Times* with a second staging of Stuart Paterson's *Uncle Vanya* translation first seen at the Royal Lyceum last year. He achieved a funny, well-designed and exhilarating piece of theatre with Sandy Neilson as Vanya balancing vigour with understatement. Glen's hallmark Scots-accented production showed conclusively (as if there were any doubt) that you don't need to sound like an upper-class Englishman to explain what life in rural Russia might be like.

From further north came Drama na h-Alba

and the Invisible Bouncers with *The Aipple Tree*, or *Craobh nan Ubhal*, a play written in Gaelic, Doric, and the American English of the oil rigs. The production was strong on visual imagery, made good use of dance and music, and was powerful in its impressionistic, snapshot creation of offshore life in the North East. Domhnall Ruadh's script provided a welcome commentary and a much needed voice to the contrasting cultures of Scotland.

Otherwise it was a mixed bag on the touring circuit. Cumbernauld Theatre produced *My Brother's Keeper* by John McKay. On its opening night in Cumbernauld, battling against a howling wind giving a little too much of the requisite headland atmosphere, this comedy about four very different men spending the night in a lighthouse only rarely achieved its full comic momentum, though later in the tour, playing in more amenable venues, Liz Carruthers' production found its natural pace and, though it could hardly be called profound, provided an enjoyable and good-natured night in the theatre.

Both Fifth Estate's *The Scapegoat*, a new play by Clive Paton seemingly about the rise to power of a military dictatorship, and New Stage Theatre Company's *Don Juan Returns from the War*, a neglected drama by Odon von Horvath, gave the impression of being intelligent, tightly written and certainly stylishly performed, but it was unclear what either was trying to say. You can't beat a clear story with obvious moral debate, as Iain Reekie's production of *Antigone* for 7:84 proved. For all that the acting was po-faced and the emotions small-scale, the power of Sophocles' narrative, coupled with strong performances by Sandy West and Pauline Knowles, won out in the end. Pen Name Theatre Company, meanwhile, produced an uneven version of Marlowe's *Doctor Faustus* that made up in energy, imagination and a couple of notably strong performances, what it lacked in balance.

Finally, benefiting from the introduction of a new low £1 concession ticket, Glasgow's Centre for Contemporary Arts enjoyed a particularly successful season of innovative European dance, with sellout performances introducing audiences to the choreographers who are set to become the major names of tomorrow.   *Mark Fisher*

Pamphleteer

The teaching and resource activity pack *Pirlie Pig and Broon Coo: Objects and Images in Scottish Language and Literature* has been produced by the National Galleries of Scotland Education Department and sponsored by the Clydesdale Bank. It is a colourful and glossy production, aimed at Standard and Higher grade English students, covering topics such as Scots Language, Gaelic and responses to it by Lowland Scots, the link between language and identity through place-names and historical objects, and painting and narration in Wilkie. It also does a helterskelter tour of Great Scottish Writers, Scott, Burns, Stevenson and MacDiarmid.

In one sense this is excellent – MacDiarmid for example has made very little impact beyond academia. On the other hand the culture portrayed is overwhelmingly male. By using Alexander Moffat's *Poet's Pub* on the cover as an image of Scottish literature, 50% of the population are visually pushed to the margins. Female Scottish teenagers need positive representations of themselves in culture/literature, not a Scottish Liberty waving a flag in the background or skulking miserably at pub doorways: Phillipson's *7 London Street* could just as easily have been used (and is in the Portrait Gallery), and would have given a more balanced representation of women's contributions to Scottish culture in the 20th Century.

I also find intriguing one of the cards headed "Representations of Scotland" where the pupil is invited to think about three images: one by Callum Colville, another of a tartan-clad chief by Raeburn, and a 'Bonnie Scotland' series postcard – the old "tartanry/Kailyard" popping up again. Surprising since these very categories have come in for some scrutiny and intense questioning about their constructions as bogeys of the Scottish popular memory. What really rankles is that somehow I can't imagine a kid frae the Home Counties on a day-trip to the V&A being asked to do some thinking about representations of England.

Another publication for use in schools is *Caa Doon the Mune* published by Angus Libraries & Museums. It ranges from "action

rhymes" for younger pupils to poems like 'Haggis Huntin frae a BMX', and stories for older pupils by William Hershaw and Mary McIntosh, all in Scots. With a glossary at the back it makes an excellent resource for children trying their hand at writing in Scots.

Also in Scots, *Rhymes frae the Ochils* by Henry Kinnard, available from the author at 2 Muirpark Road, Kinross, KY13 7AT (£2), poetry in Scots and English in a traditional style reflecting the author's rural background. In contrast *The Glasgow Gospel* (St Andrews Press, £3.95), translated by Jamie Stewart, has a very urban feel. I can't help feeling that there must still be some guid sauls who would balk at Jesus saying "Right then Jimmy, juist you dae the same" after telling the parable of the Good Samaritan! Also from Glasgow, Jimmy Millar's *Tenements as Tall as Ships* (Govan Workspace Ltd, £3.75), a collection of short stories written between the 1950s and '80s. Very much of their place and time – Govan and shipbuilding – and as a result cannot but occasionally become nostalgic. But for all that it's well-written and enjoyable.

The Unit for the Study of Government in Scotland, based at Edinburgh University, has produced four booklets (£3 each) on various constitutional and political issues. They cover a wide spectrum of opinions, and are not too academic as most are based on transcripts of conversations rather than papers. Available at the moment: *What Scotland Wants: Ten Years On* – a conference in 1989, participants including Neil MacCormick, Alan Lawson and Neal Ascherson; *Financing Home Rule* (1990); *Asking the People: The Referendum and Constitutional Change* (1992) includes 'How to Run a Referendum' by Simon Osborne of the Electoral Reform Society. You never know, it may come in handy… Also *Women in Scottish Politics*, which has very useful statistics for comparison with other European countries, and analysis of policies for increasing the participation of women in politics.

The Clocktower Press has been rebuilt on Orkney (24 Dundas Street, Stromness, KW16 3BZ) and has resumed production of very reasonably priced booklets, some tasters of larger work to come. *Past Tense: Four Stories from a Novel* by Irvine Welsh is an extract from his novel *Train-spotting* to be published later this year by Secker. And destined it is to trample on the sacred territory held until now by Glaswegian novelists – no longer will general urban decay and misery in modern ScotLit be the exclusive preserve of the few. *Past Tense* has it all – living HIV positive in a multi-story in Granton, the drugs, the violence etc. Anyway read the booklet before deciding whether to shell out on one of Secker's pricey paperback originals. Also in the same series *The Collected Works* of Brent Hodgson – if you have enjoyed this New Zealand dairy expert's previous appearances in *Chapman* you'll like this. Including West of Scotland haiku like: "a rammy ootside/ whit aboot? fuckin Peter/ dropt the carry-oot". Both pamphlets cost £1.50 including postage – cheques to be made out to D. McLean.

Cusp by Hugh Clark Small – a booklet of short stories (£2.50 made out to author, 2 Murray Place, Aberdour, Fife, KY3 0XD) – varies wildly. I liked 'Above the World', though not his eccentric use of the fullstop. *Hepworth: A Celebration* is an anthology of poetry on the life, work and sculpture-garden of Barbara Hepworth. Poets include Sylvia Kantaris, Willam Oxley, and Philip Gross (Westwords Publications £4.50). *Memorabilia* by Colin Flack (Taxus Press £5.95): I like the poems, loathe the Memorabilia – pages of airline ticket receipts and twee notes between lovers. Willam Scammell's fifth collection *Bleeding Heart Yard* is published by Peterloo Poets at £6.95 – well worth getting hold of to experience his confident use of language and range of subject matter:

Tall dogs with silky hair
slipped moorings by the Aga
gliding up to my strange scent:
the squash-faced semi-precious cat
subsided into a hump; and you
sat down, oblique and fine as
an old fashioned stroke of the pen.

Sean Rafferty is mentioned in *From Wood to Ridge* as one of the best-known poets of his generation during the 1930s. After being widely published in Scottish magazines, he went silent until the '70s, but in 1982 *PN Review* ran a retrospective of his work. His work is finely crafted and structured with a broad range of subject matter, and *Poems 1940-1982* is now available from 132 Hassell

Street, Newcastle under Lyme, Staffordshire, ST5 IBB (£4.50 inc p&p).

I'm sure it is a lack on my part but the poems in *The Chromoscope* by Jenny Johnson (Mammon Press, £?) just did not grab me – perhaps because I don't meditate or wave crystals about. On second thoughts, good poetry should be able to covey its subject however alien to the reader. *New Pastorals* by Robert Etty (The Frogmore Press £2.50): the title says it all – musings on rural realities today, in verse. *Alum Rock Poems* by Michael Crowshaw (Making Waves, £3) breathes life and voice into such diverse beings as Humpty Dumpty and Ulysses. *Himalayan Fish* by Cliff Forshaw (22 East Dulwich Road, London, SE22 9AX, £5.95) is dominated – "India was a drug I couldn't quit" – by poems about India and Mr Forshaw's sweeping generalisations about modern life. Let's just say he's not afraid to leap towards the big things.

From Merlin: *George Washington and other poems* by Roger Mason (£3.95) is fine if you like your poetry doggerelly. *Album* by George Ambridge (£2.95) contains old-fashioned poetry and sometimes reactionary sentiments. *Autumn Leaves* by Margery Green (£4.50) refreshingly makes no claims for this to be poetry – just versifying, which she claims any literate person can do… Thankfully the result in her hands is unpretentious and jolly, which is a nice change.

Finally four titles from the National Poetry Foundation. *Metaphor and Cold Water* Alan Davis, *Strange December Warmth* Ron Woodruff, *The Clear-Out* by Alan Barrett, and *A View from Suburbia* by Patrick Taylor, all £4.50. Four authors, but I would probably say in a blind test they were by the same person: they are flat and lacking in interest to those not the author or relation. Occasionally, in their little-England-reminiscence mode, they sway to the arguably racist ("'Man, ain't I just lucky/ My skin's dermatographical!'/ How's that for positive thinking?", Alan Davis 'A Leg of Verse', on a black woman poet). The blurbs can cause accidental interest – especially the poet who claims that he indulges in "spasmodic athletics". On hearing this our assistant editor threw himself around the office attempting to emulate the condition… the volunteers enjoyed it anyway. *Mary Gordon*

Catalogue

Selected Poems of Henryson & Dunbar (ed Priscilla Bawcutt & Felicity Riddy, SAP, £9.75) contains a wide range of both these great poets' work, with scholarly annotations, a book to keep alongside Walter Bower's *Scotichronicon*, of which it's time to welcome volume six of Donald Watt's edition (AUP, £40). A history of Scotland composed at Inchcolm in the 15th century, this volume presents Bower's books XI and XII, covering the period 1286–1319, in a dual text for the delight of Latin scholars and general readers alike. And it *is* a delight: the accounts are lucid, the background carefully explained, and there is a narrative drive behind it of rare quality.

If the story of Edward I's scheming and conniving is depressingly familiar, Bower's discourse is refreshingly alien: it was written in a relatively stable period, at a time when Scotland was governed by Scots and Bower could confidently look at the English with scorn. I applaud the painstaking scholarship which has gone into the translation, but I also suspect that an edition shorn of its Latin and footnotes, available at a substantially lower price, might do well in the market. A flavour:

...the magnates and powerful men of the kingdom, intoxicated by a stream of envy, seditiously entered a secret plot against the guardian under the guise of expressions of virgin-innocence but with their tails tied together. ... Why is covetous envy so much in control in Scotland? (p93)

David Craig's *King Cameron* (Carcanet, £12.95), a historical novel set in early- to mid-nineteenth century Highland Scotland, seems terribly pale and worthy by comparison: a 'factional' account of Lochaber carpenter Angus Cameron against the background of the clearances, the history and the patient style of narrative makes it good reading for school-age people.

Venus Peter Saves The Whale (Christopher Rush/Mairi Hedderwick, Canongate, £6.95) is unequivocally children's reading, engaging, fantastical and concise; focussed on the boyish adventures of Peter, I wonder whether girls will find it relevant. George Garson's *Orkney All The Way Through* (John Donald, £8.95) tries oh-so-hard to be jolly and matey, the overwrought language, beating the reader over the head with metaphors and adjectives, simply makes one want to move one's head elsewhere, to the delicious purity of language in George Mackay Brown's novel *Vinland* (John Murray, 14.95) for example: the story of Ranald Sigmundson's voyage through life, a stowaway when Leif Ericsson finds the Vinland of the title, later a prosperous farmer, finally called back to the sea 900 years ago. Mackay Brown's characteristic simplicity is, equally characteristically, never simplistic as he coaxes metaphor from everyday experience. GMB fans will be grateful to Osamu Yamada, Hilda Spear and David S Robb, who have collaborated on *The Contribution to Literature of Orcadian Writer George Mackay Brown* (Edwin Mellen Press, £?), which combines a brief (27 page) introduction to his work with a mightily extensive bibliography.

John R Allen's novel *Green Heritage* (Ardo Publishing, £12.50) is a novel from, though not necessarily of, a bygone age. An account of farming in the North-West from the late '30s, it is trenchant, partisan, and well-written with a good ear for language. In Frederic Lindsay's *After the Stranger Came* (Andre Deutsch, £13.99), the wife of a politically incorrect academic falls victim to one of his associates (as does said academic) in a marvellous literary thriller. A scent of Burroughs in the handling of time among other things, though without the narcissistic nihilism.

Jessie Kesson's lively and compelling *The White Bird Passes* has just been re-issued as a Virago Modern Classic (£5.99) so the saintly can now ignore Norman MacCaig's advice ("Beg, borrow or steal this book") and *buy* a copy! Also from Virago, *The Young Person's Action Guide to Animal Rights* by Barbara James (£3.99) underlines the topic's queasy morality and raises serious questions without forcing answers down the reader's throat. *Refusing Holy Orders: Women and Fundamentalism in Britain* (Virago, £8.99) covers similarly contentious ground: editors Gita Sahgal and Nira Yuval-Davis include material on Judaism and Christianity as well as the more familiar questions surrounding Islam, although the chance to make an illuminating comparison between Southern Irish Catholic fundamentalism and Ulster protestant fundamentalism has been missed – Ulster is the one corner of the British Isles left unexamined.

On the premise that "Death has always been as fatal in Glasgow as it is anywhere else" and "...there is a distinctive 'Glasgow' attitude towards the phenomenon of death..." Jimmy Black has come up with *The Glasgow Graveyard Guide* (St Andrew Press, £4.95). Also from St Andrew, though larger and more lavish, is Marianna Lines' *Sacred Stones, Sacred Places* (£19.95), taking a particular interest in the Pictish and Celtic carvings which are such an important part of Scottish heritage. Kin, in that respect, is *Six Scottish Burghs* (Canongate, £10.95), which sees Andy MacMillan, Professor of Architecture at Glasgow University, take an illustrated stroll round Kelso, Thurso, Elgin, Stirling, Paisley and Dumfries. Reprinted in a revised, greener edition (St Andrew Press, £4.50), is Rennie McOwan's *Walks in the Trossachs and the Rob Roy Country*. Good to know what you didn't see on all those mist-shrouded hills.

Tony Troon's *The Best of The Scotsman Diary* (Mainstream, £6.99) has its amusing moments, but this kind of book inevitably suffers from a lack of currency (as in affairs, that is). David S Robb's *Scotnotes* guide to *The Prime of Miss Jean Brodie* contains a series of essays on various aspects of Muriel Spark's classic novel (ASLS, £?) for school and further education students. In similar vein, though less appetising visually, is *Four Glsgow Writers* (ed Peter Maclaren, for Strathclyde Region Education Dept, £?), a classroom resource on Morgan/McIlvanney/Lochhead/Spence. In response, as it were, *Young Writers in Strathclyde* (also from Strathclyde Region ED, £?) is a collection of writing from pupils from the region's schools. *The Scottish Society of Artists: the First 100 Years* (Scottish Society of Artists, £15) requires little elaboration. Containing many full-colour reproductions and an essay by Cordelia Oliver, it is excellent value for money. Likewise *Tales from the Coast*, a selection of some of the best, most innovative and experimental fiction from West Coast Magazine (Taranis, £4.99).

Carnage: New Writing from Europe (ed Michael Blackburn, Sunk Island, £5) contains all the geographical diversity the title implies, from Spain to Finland, whose Bo Carpelan

proves you can be poet and Academic Librarian without the claustrophobic self-pity which characterises certain English specimens of the genre. From the same neck of the forest, Robin Fulton and White Pine Press have produced two volumes of Nordic poetry: one, *Olav Hauge – Selected Poems* focussed on the single laconic, wry Norwegian writer, the other *Four Swedish Poets – Transtromer, Strom, Sjogren, Espmark* giving a taste of a broader range of Swedish writing.

Speaking of broad ranges, *The Bright Field* is an anthology of contemporary poetry from Wales (Carcanet, £9.95). Editor Meic Stephens (of *Poetry Wales*) asked contributors to make their own selections, and though I have my doubts about how broad Stephens' selection of contributors is, age, gender, social background-wise, the standard is high. I liked Douglas Houston's 'Taliesin: Interim Report', linking the silver-tongued bard to contemporary advertising copywriters; Paul Groves' 'Making Love to Marilyn Monroe', which you might call 'ode to a blow-up doll' in a tackier mood. The range of subject matter is perhaps *too* wide, making the whole seem over-diffuse. Broad range is a feature of Michael Hulse's *Eating Strawberries in the Necropolis* (Harvill, £5.95), but here it is a positive virtue – it's one person's broad range – making for an immensely resonant collection of poetry.

Somhairle: Dàin is Deilbh is an 80th birthday celebration for Sorley MacLean (ed Angus Peter Campbell, Acair, £?) largely, though not entirely, in Gaelic, with contributions from many of the Gaedhealtacht's best-known writers and extensively illustrated: a fine tribute. Where better to mention a valuable new resource for Gaelic learners: Henry Cyril Dieckhoff's *Prounouncing Dictionary of Scottish Gaelic* (Gairm, £7.50), based on oral records of the Glengarry dialect gathered during the last century. Finally, Angus Peter Campbell, has a collection of his own: *The Greatest Gift* (Fountain Publishing, £7.95). Like Michael Hulse, Campbell plays language as a resonant instrument while retaining a strong sense of his own identity. "A post-Presley Gael", as the cover puts it, surprisingly there is no Gaelic inside. Never mind. What *is* inside establishes Campbell as an important new voice.

Notes on Contributors

Gerry Cambridge lives in Ayrshire. In his twenties worked as a freelance journalist/photographer, specialising in natural history; now co-edits *Spectrum,* and has two collections of poetry looking for a publisher.

David Daiches: Emeritus Professor of English at University of Sussex and former Director of the Institute for Advanced Studies at Edinburgh. Has published some 45 books of criticism, history and biography once a regular contributor to *The New Yorker.*

William I Elliott/Kazuo Kawamura: Colleagues in literature faculty of Kanto Sakuim University, Yokohama. The former a poet who also directs the Kanto Poetry center; the latter, writing on Shelley and Yeats, has given up jogging for rapid walking.

Norman Garlock: b Kirkwall, 1957; proud graduate of Newbattle Abbey. Currently studying Literature in Aberdeen University. Co-founder of *Mica* literary magazine.

Mary Gordon: Born Pietermaritzburg of Latvian, Scots, and Huguenot ancestry. Still recovering from her Scottish Education - all those who suffered the *Gallery* anthology during Higher English will understand...

George Gunn: well-known around Scotland as radical poet and playwright.

Alex Hamilton: 'Hysteria' is an excerpt from his forthcoming novel *Stretch Marks.*

Maggi Higgins: currently studying literature at Strathclyde University; has also attended Glasgow School of Art. She has had illustrations and poetry published previously.

Jeremy Hughes teaches in a college of further education and prison in Wales. He has been published widely.

Alexander Innes: Born Edinburgh 1948. Started writing through the EU Continuing Education Creative Writing Workshops run by Sandy Hutchison.

Shirley Geok-lin Lim, winner of the Commonwealth Poetry Prize in 1980, teaches at the University of California Santa Barbera.

Maurice Lindsay: Once Programme Controller for Border Television. His many publications include *The Burns Encyclopaedia* and *History of Scottish Literature.* Mercat Press publish his *Collected Poems 1940-1990.*

Morag McCarron: Born Fife, studied in Edinburgh, currently lives in Italy, teaching English at the University of Urbino.

aonghas macneacail is working on a TV documentary at the moment. Recent books *Rock and Water* (Polygon); *An Seachnadh* (Lines Review Editions).

David McVey: Unrepentantly a native of Kirkintilloch, works for Scripture Union in Glasgow.

John Manson: Crofter three years, teacher thirty-one years, now translator and critic.

Graham Dunstan Martin teaches French at Edinburgh University. Novels include *Half a Glass of Moonshine* (Unwin Heinemann) and *Timeslip.*

Edwin Morgan's most recent book is *Cyrano de Bergerac,* a translation of Rostand's play into Scots (Carcanet,1992)

William Neill has published several collections of verse which others sometimes describe as poetry.

Catherine Orr: Lives in Glasgow where she works as a physiotherapist. A late starter to poetry she has had work published in *New Writing Scotland* and *Scottish Child.*

Mario Relich: Course tutor in the Arts for the Open University in Scotland

Maureen Sangster: Born Aberdeen 1954, now lives in Fife. Poet and adult education tutor published in various anthologies and magazines.

Kenneth Steven: Currently teaching English in Norwegian Lappland, following literary studies at Glasgow University. Fantasy novel *The Unborn* due out in July.

Shuntaro Tanikawa: Born Tokyo 1931, refused to attend university, published first book of poems at 21. Shaped the character of modern Japanese poetry away from haiku and waka and French influences towards the directions of post-war American poetry.

Ruth Thomas: Born 1967, lives in Edinburgh and works as a freelance journalist and copy-editor. Also writes children's stories.

Billy Watt: Born Greenock, writes fiction and poetry. Now lives and works in West Lothian.

Sheena Wellington: Dundee-born singer, songwriter and broadcaster, active agitator in the cause of Scotland's songs, music and freedom. Latest recording *Clearsong.*

David Winwood: Lives in Eire, and after the 'emotional turmoil' of relocating, is experiencing 'pleasing periods of detachment'.